Angels and Fire:

Yefet ben 'Eli HaLewi on Dani'el and Nahum

D.S. Margoliouth, trans.
Hartwig Hirschfeld, trans.
Y. Yaron, ed.

Text of Daniel from the New JPS Translation of the
Tanakh

al-Qirqisani Center for the Promotion of Karaite Studies

Library of Congress Card Number: 00-103639

ISBN 0970077505

Editor's Note

Yefet ibn Ali Hallewi lived in the last quarter of the tenth century. He was born and lived in Basra Iraq for a large portion of his life. However, at some point, he moved to Jerusalem, where he died. Yefet was one of the most influential Karaite commentators of his age. He wrote an exhaustive commentary of the Tanach, and provided a translation for it, all in Arabic, the common tongue. Yefet's commentaries are infused with theological, legal, grammatical and historical insights, as well as polemics against Rabbanism, Christianity and Islam. It is commonly held that his commentaries were influential in both Rabbanite and Karaite circles, including the work of the famous Rabbanite commentator Avraham ibn Ezra. Nothing more is known about his life.

The reader may note certain differences between the text of Daniel chosen to accompany the commentary of Yefet ibn Ali, and the text of the commentary itself. This is due to differences in translation between the New JPS Translation of Daniel and the passages translated by D.S. Margoulith. Decisions were made at certain points to reconcile the text of the commentary to the translation; however, in general, it was felt that the translation of Margoulith was best left untouched, as it most closely fit with the commentary of Yefet ibn Ali Hallewi. Furthermore, the differences in translation often bring to light many interesting choices made by the various translators.

Congregation B'nei Yisra'el
Daly City, San Francisco
- *Y. Yaron*

The Book of Daniel

The book of Daniel. This book has been attributed to Daniel in particular because it contains an account of his history and prophecy. It contains eleven chapters.

If we add up the span of years covered by this book, they total up to sixty-seven: seventy years were occupied by the reigns of Nebuchadnezzar, Evil-Merodach, and Belshazzar; all of which come within our narrative, except the first seven years of Nebuchadnezzar, as we will see below. This leaves sixty-three years. Add to this the one year of Darius and the three years of Cyrus; the result is a total of sixty-seven years.

The reign of Jehoiakim was divided into three parts: a) four years during which he was subject to the king of Egypt; b) three years during which he was subject to the king of Babylon (2 Kings 24.1); [c] three years during which he was independent.] During these three years, the king of Babylon was occupied with his Eastern expedition. After he had rested a little, he attacked him (in the tenth year of his reign), besieged him with his army, took his city, took him prisoner, and carried away many captives with part of the vessels of the house of God (as above).

¹In the third year of the reign of King Jehoiakim of Judah, King Nebuchadnezzar of Babylon came to Jerusalem and laid siege to it.

In the third year: not in the tenth year, for the following reason: Jehoiakim had originally been subject to the king of Egypt. Then, he became subject to the king of Babylon. Thus, seven years passed; and - since he rebelled against the king of Babylon after this, and became an independent king, who paid homage to no other - the writer can say *in the third year of the reign of Jehoiakim king of Israel,* dating from the time when he became independent. The proof of our theory of the division of Jehoiakim's reign into three parts is the statement in 2 Chronicles 36.4, that the king of Egypt took Jehoahaz, brother of Jehoiakim, sent him to Egypt, and made Jehoiakim king in his stead. Now, we know that he remained subject to the king of Egypt four years, and that the king of Babylon came to the throne in the fourth year of Jehoiakim; see Jeremiah 10-15.1, where it is stated that the first year of Nebuchadnezzar was the fourth of Jehoiakim. In that year, the king of Babylon fought with the king of Egypt, who was encamped on the banks of the Euphrates (see Jeremiah. 1. c.), when Syria fell into his hands (2 Kings 24.7). Now, Jehoiakim became subject to the king of Babylon in the fifth year of his reign.

came to Jerusalem and laid siege to it: he was not satisfied with sending an army against him, but led the army himself. Had Jehoiakim come out to him, he would not have besieged the city. Jehoiakim, however, would not submit, but locked the gates and withstood the siege, thinking that the king of Babylon would grow tired and desist. The king, however, maintained the siege until he took the city.
2. Either he stormed the city, as some think, or the people

6

may have opened the gates. The latter is more likely, as no battle is mentioned. Jehoiakim, we are told, died outside Jerusalem. Either the king of Babylon tormented him until he died, or he was killed [in some other way], or he may have killed himself.

²The Lord delivered King Jehoiakim of Judah into his power, together with some of the vessels of the House of God, and he brought them to the land of Shinar to the house of his god; he deposited the vessels in the treasury of his god. ³Then the king ordered Ashpenaz, his chief officer, to bring some Israelites of royal descent and of the nobility -

and he brought them to the land of Shinar: The king of Babylon carried away captive more than three thousand men. They are mentioned in Jeremiah 52.28.

he deposited the vessels into the treasury of his god: observe that we are not told the *number* of the vessels, nor their material (gold, silver, or brass); doubtless they were different vessels from those taken away with Jehoiakim (2 Chronicles 36.10); they were not used by him, but put together in a safe place. Had he attempted to use them, God would not have permitted it, even as He did not permit Belshazzar, but showed serious signs [of His disapproval].

3, 4. He ordered the chief of his ministers, who was responsible for the captive Israelites, to choose from the youths of Israel without fixing a number. He was to look out for all who possessed these characteristics, and to take them, however few or many of them there might be.

of the children of Israel: i.e. of those who were not of royal stock, or of the children of the nobles, but *of the common people*. He did not care whether or not such a person came from the common people, when found to possess these qualities. This is to show that talented people are not affected by the lowness of their station.

And he ordered him to take the best looking of them. It would not be seemly that a person who was unsightly should

8

stand in his court; such people must be handsome, comely and fair.

—[4]youths without blemish, handsome, proficient in all wisdom, knowledgeable and intelligent, and capable of serving in the royal palace

proficient in all wisdom: not wisdom in the Torah concerning 'unclean' and 'clean,' or 'sacrifices.' The king would not be interested in that. He wanted people learned in all academic studies and subjects.

knowledgeable: most probably knowledge, like Solomon's, in the different departments of philosophy. The children of Israel were never lacking in philosophy, but always taught it to their children. Even in the times of their idolatry and wickedness, there never ceased to be those among them who sought wisdom and knowledge.

and understanding teaching: knowing the way to instruct others in their knowledge. Not every scholar makes a good teacher.

So he chose all those who possessed all these virtues and desirable qualities. Since this was done at the time described, it was unlikely that there would be [many] young men among them possessing these qualities.

those who would be able to stand in the king's presence: i.e. force of patience to stand before the king, and to abstain from expectorating, spitting, etc.

—and teach them the writings and the language of the Chaldeans. ⁵The king allotted daily rations to them from the king's food and from the wine he drank. They were to be educated for three years, ᵃ⁻at the end of which they⁻ᵃ were to enter the king's service.⁶Among them were the Judahites Daniel, Hananiah, Mishael and Azariah. ⁷The chief officer gave them new names; he named Daniel Belteshazzar, Hananiah Shadrach, Mishael Meshach, and Azariah Abed-nego.

and teach them the writings and the language: This was so they would be able to write it and speak it. Naturally, they would not know either.

If Ashpenaz, himself, had not possessed many of these gifts and understood them, the king would not have given him this order.

The king's object in taking these youths was twofold: (1) to gratify his desire for men of knowledge; for it is the custom of high-minded kings to have scholars trained in their courts; (2) to be able to boast before the nations that in his court are the greatest men in the world.

5. It was not the king's purpose to corrupt their religion, as he endeavored to do in the story of the image which he set up. Rather, he wanted them to have a suitable diet - which would make them grow, and give them a healthy appearance. So he made their rations like his own: the best food and drink.

He also planned to train them for three years, so they would come before the king looking healthy, familiar with the writing and language, and all that was desired of them.

6. These four are mentioned on account of their abstaining from the king's food, and the rest of their achievements. Among them were some of the royalty, whom

---

ᵃ⁻ *Or "and some of them."*
⁻ᵃ *Or "and some of them."*

11

the Scripture does not mention. Had these four been royalty, he would have said, 'there were among them of the royalty,' mentioning their rank. This disproves the view that Isaiah 39.2 refers to these.

7. He gave them Chaldean names; possibly *names of honor*, since *Belteshazar* is the name of Nebuchadnezzar's God *(inf 4.5)*; the rest may be so too.

⁸Daniel resolved not to defile himself with the king's food or the wine he drank, so he sought permission of the chief officer not to defile himself,

8. Daniel refused to eat the king's food or consume his drink, whatever the consequences might be; staking his life, just as he staked it in his prayer, and as Hananiah, Mishael, and Azariah staked theirs when they would not bow down to the image. It is quite impossible that Daniel would have staked it for something inconsequential, as some irreligious people have said, whom we have answered in our commentary on the commandment.

not to defile himself: not, 'he would not eat;' meaning that he would not eat a meat originally clean, but one that was defiled by [coming in contact with] uncleanness. He did not differentiate between the meat (consisting of animals slaughtered by Gentiles) and the drink. It is possible that the meat was not from a forbidden animal, nor the wine naturally forbidden; but he refused it because it was prepared by Gentiles, though it was free from all taint of uncleanness. This was because he regarded the grape-juice as the original state [i.e. he regarded the wine as a transformation of grape-juice], and refused to touch that which had come in contact with uncleanness.

The chief of the eunuchs is Ashpenaz. He said, 'My LORD, do not give me, I beg of you, food and drink which will not benefit me.' But Ashpenaz gave him an answer which robbed him of all hope that his request would be granted.

13

⁹and God disposed the chief officer to be kind and compassionate toward Daniel. ¹⁰The chief officer said to Daniel, "I fear that my lord the king, who allotted food and drink to you, will notice that you look out of sorts, unlike the other youths of your age—and you will put my life[b] in jeopardy with the king." ¹¹Daniel replied to the guard whom the chief officer had put in charge of Daniel, Hananiah, Mishael and Azariah,

9. **kind and compassionate** comprise two periods; the first, sc. *favor*, had been shown previously, and consisted in various acts of kindness shown to Daniel which he does not describe at length; the second, *compassion* took place at that particular time. It consisted in Ashpenaz doing him no harm or violence, nor informing the king, but excusing him as follows.

10. Ashpenaz tells him that he refuses only out of fear for his life. If the king should send for them, wishing to observe their condition; and he saw that their faces were different from the others, he would inquire about the matter. When, on inquiring, he found out about the change in their food, the blame would fall on Ashpenaz, while they would not be reprehended.

according to your joy: because the wise are continually joyful and merry, because knowledge wastes the body and destroys it.

MtbyH, like bVH in Ezekiel 18.7.

11. As the chief eunuch would not grant his request, and he had bound himself to stake his life upon it, he tried speaking to the man who provided his food, in case *he* might do this for them, and try them, as we will explain presently.

---

[b] *Lit. "head."*

14

¹²"Please test your servants for ten days, giving us legumes to eat and water to drink. ¹³Then compare our appearance with that of the youths who eat of the king's food, and do with your servants as you see fit." ¹⁴He agreed to this plan of theirs, and tested them for ten days. ¹⁵When the ten days were over, they looked better and healthier than all the youths who were eating of the king's food. ¹⁶So the guard kept on removing their food, and the wine they were supposed to drink, and gave them legumes.

12. **test your servants for ten days.** A short time, of which little account is usually taken; in order to facilitate the matter, and make it easier to accomplish.

13, 14. He accepted their proposal. Afterwards, he examined them, and found them healthier than the others who had been eating the king's food and drinking his wine. The Creator, who set in the grain something to supply the place of meat, and similarly in the water, must have done this. Those who did not refuse the king's food, as did Daniel and his friends, must have either argued that they were excused, and that it was impossible for them to resist the Sultan, or they did so because they did not care about what is lawful and unlawful. To these God sent leanness into their bodies, so that they did not fatten. This proves that God cares for His saints who are willing to suffer death for His law's sake.

When the ten days were over, when he found that their appearance had improved, he continued their diet for a period of three years.

16. He profited by the provisions and took them for himself in secret, without telling Ashpenaz.

gbtp includes bread and dainties. The word may be divided into two: tp bread, and gb dainties,' i.e. bread and meat. **Pulse [legumes]** is the substitute for it.

They took wheat for bread, and some other grains to cook, such as lentils, rice, peas, and beans, and they drank

15

water. Of course they took grain that was not defiled; and water out of the river in clean vessels, as they wished.

¹⁷God made all four of these young men intelligent and proficient in all writings and wisdom, and Daniel had understanding of visions and dreams of all kinds. ¹⁸When the time the king had set for their presentation had come, the chief officer presented them to Nebuchadnezzar. ¹⁹The king spoke with them, and of them all none was equal to Daniel, Hananiah, Mishael and Azariah; so these entered the king's service.

17. They already had the wisdom described above; which God Almighty increased during these days with additional wisdom, in all learning and philosophy known by the sages and Chaldees. Daniel surpassed them through the possession of certain divine gifts, such as the interpretation of all visions. The Chaldees did not understand dreams. This was not *confined* to Daniel, since Hananiah and the rest were distinguished as well. Daniel, however, was the most eminent. This was all the Creator's purpose (**God gave them**), compare *inf.* 11.21 and Proverbs 20.6.

18. At the end of the three years, during which the king had commanded that they be nourished and instructed in the 'writing and language,' the **Chief of the Eunuchs** brought them before him, and the king began to examine them in the different departments of science. He found none among the Jewish youths like Daniel and his companions (**all of them** refers to the Jews). This was owing to what was mentioned before -- God's bestowing on them clear intelligence. Next, he tells us that they were ten times better than the king's sages. Either this is a [figure of speech or else a] real number, and we are to infer that the king called all his sages before him in their presence, and told them to ask one another questions, while he heard what passed between them. Doubtless, he himself was a sage and understood the discourse; and he comprehended what passed between them, and how they surpassed all his sages ten times in breadth of knowledge. Perhaps, there were men among his sages who

17

had been studying science all their lives until they had grown old, who yet had not obtained the knowledge of these four. All this was in order that God might exalt His servants who were sunk to the lowest depth, and yet they had clung to His religion and not indulged themselves with eating unlawful food, but had eaten grain instead. Among the philosophers there must have arisen mutterings against certain meats, 'Woe to him that eats defiled food and the preparation of the Gentiles - defiling his soul and removing it from holiness, and withdrawing it from God Almighty. Woe to him who finds ways of explaining away the commandments, eats forbidden foods, and drinks the Gentile drinks, with creeping things and abominations among them.' There is no difference between wine and any other drink, all of them being *mashqiym*. And no person during the Captivity can possibly eat the preparation of anyone whom he knows to be unfaithful in his observances in the matter of preparation of meats, so that his food is unclean and impure. Such cases are referred to in Leviticus 20.25 and Psalms 74.10.

²⁰Whenever the king put a question to them requiring wisdom and understanding, he found them to be ten times better than all the magicians and exorcists throughout his realm. ²¹Daniel was there until the first year of King Cyrus.

II

In the second year of the reign of Nebuchadnezzar, Nebuchadnezzar had a dream; his spirit was agitated, yet he ^{a-} was overcome by^{-a} sleep.

21. **Continued [was there]**: i.e. Daniel was in the Sultan's kingdom until the first year of Cyrus - the time when the Israelites were set free to go to the Holy Land and build the Temple; when he was set free from the duties of government and retired into religious life. He had grown old by then. As for his companions, he tells us nothing about them after the story of the image.

II

1. Just as we said that the phrase 'third year of the reign of Jehoiakim' did not refer to Jehoiakim's reign literally, so this again does not refer to Nebuchadnezzar's *reign,* as Daniel is the person who interpreted the dream. Plainly, it must refer to something else. Some have supposed it to be the *second year of Jehoiakim's captivity,* which is unlikely, because Daniel had no office until after three years (see 1.5, which shows that he licensed them after three years). Others have referred it to the *fall of Jerusalem,* imagining that he did not consider himself king until he had subdued Israel; which is not improbable. To

---

^{a-} *Meaning of Heb. uncertain others "could not."*
^{-a} *Meaning of Heb. uncertain others "could not."*

19

my mind, what is most probable is that it means [the second year] *after he had become king of the entire world (inf.* 2.38). Now, it is well known that Nebuchadnezzar took Jerusalem before he took Tyre, and Tyre before he took Egypt. It is most probable that he took Egypt in the thirtieth year of his reign. This is shown by Ezekiel 29.11, 'neither will it be inhabited forty years,' etc. (cp. 13). Now, it was God's decree concerning all of the captives that they should remain in their present condition seventy years, made up by Nebuchadnezzar, his son, and his son's son (Jeremiah 25.11); none of them returning to his country until after the *completion* of these seventy years. Now Egypt was the last of his conquests, as no other king stood before him except for Pharaoh. Therefore, the words **in the second year** refer to the thirty-second year of his reign, thirteen years after the destruction of the Temple. In that year, Ezekiel saw the form of the Temple (49.1). Nebuchadnezzar took the Holy City and burnt the Temple in the seventeenth year of his reign; and, if Nebuchadnezzar saw the dream in the thirty-second year of his reign, then thirteen years must have passed since the destruction of the Temple. Therefore, the appearance of the dream would have taken place in the fourteenth year [after its destruction].

Dreamed dreams. There was only one. Our view of this phrase is that he says **dreams** because the dream contains five subjects; i.e. it encompasses the account of four kingdoms and of the empire of Israel. The same expression is used of Joseph's dream (Genesis 37.7), before he saw the second dream, and that again is because the first dream contained three subjects.

His spirit was agitated, because he awoke and forgot the dream, and tried to remember what he had seen, but could not remember it at all. Then he slept again.

Note that there is a difference between the dream of

20

Pharaoh and that of Nebuchadnezzar in two respects: 1. Pharaoh saw his dream at the end of the night (Genesis 41.8), whereas Nebuchadnezzar saw his in the middle of the night (his sleep *was* upon him); 2. Pharaoh remembered his dream, whereas Nebuchadnezzar forgot his. The reason of this was that Pharaoh's *dream was realized after a short time,* whereas Nebuchadnezzar's is not yet fully realized. Consequently, as Pharaoh's dream was realized after a short interval, God Almighty did not allow him to forget it. However, as Nebuchadnezzar's was not to be realized until after a long period, God caused him to forget it, so that when the dream was told to him, its retelling might be evidence of the its correct interpretation.

²The king ordered the magicians, exorcists, sorcerers, and Chaldeans to be summoned in order to tell the king what he had dreamed. They came and stood before the king, ³and the king said to them, "I have had a dream and ^{b-}I am full of anxiety^{-b} to know what I have dreamed." ⁴The Chaldeans spoke to the king in Aramaic, "O king, live forever! Relate the dream to your servants, and we will tell its meaning." ⁵The king said in reply to the Chaldeans, "I hereby decree: If you will not make the dream and its meaning known to me, you shall be torn limb from limb and your houses confiscated.^c ⁶But if you tell the dream and its meaning, you shall receive from me gifts, presents, and great honor; therefore, tell me the dream and its meaning."

2. These Chaldeans professed to own a certain wisdom. There was no order left, professing to reveal secrets, which Nebuchadnezzar did not summon, demanding that they should tell him the dream which he had forgotten.

3. He desired them to tell him the dream (see ver. 2).

4. Possibly he spoke to them first in some other language than the Aramaic, but afterwards addressed them in Aramaic, as they addressed him. Then they said: *Tell us the dream that we may tell you the interpretation of it.* They did not say, 'We cannot tell you the dream.'

5. He said, 'First I asked you for the dream; but, as you are not satisfied with that, I ask you now for the dream and its interpretation. And if you will not show me the dream and its interpretation, you will he hewed in pieces, i.e. your flesh will be cut up, and your houses become confiscate to the Sultan.

6. 'But, if you show me the dream and its interpretation, I will give you fine clothes, money, and beautiful presents, and high honors will be bestowed upon you; but only after you

---

^{b-} *Meaning uncertain; or "turned into ruins."*
^{-b} *Meaning uncertain; or "turned into ruins."*
^c *Lit. "tell the king's matter."*

have told me the dream and its interpretation.'

When they heard his promise and his threat, and could find no deliverer, they repeated their answer a second time.

[7]Once again they answered, "Let the king relate the dream to his servants, and we will tell its meaning." [8]The king said in reply, "It is clear to me that you are playing for time, since you see that I have decreed [9]that if you do not make the dream known to me, there is but one verdict for you. You have conspired to tell me something false and fraudulent until circumstances change; so relate the dream to me, and I will then know that you can tell its meaning."

7. 'We stand by our first answer; we undertake to *interpret* it.' Again they would not say 'We cannot tell you the dream.' When he saw them... he first demanded of them the dream without promising them or threatening them; ... afterwards, he demanded of them the dream and its interpretation, and made them a promise. When they repeated their answer about the interpretation, instead of saying ' We are unable,' he said something different to them.

8, 9. **You are playing for time**: i.e. you are making the time pass, and you imagine that I will refrain from asking you, and that you will leave me troubled in thought, with my spirit distressed, while you don't care. This is because you see that the *dream has fled from me* and I cannot remember it.

There is but, one verdict for you: i.e. one judgment; I will make no difference between you; let no one imagine that I will spare you or any one of you. Others interpret: *You are all agreed on one thing,* i.e. to say, 'Tell us the dream, and we will interpret it,' and not to tell me the dream.

false and fraudulent: i.e. if you do not tell me the dream, then you will not tell me its interpretation either. You only say 'We will interpret the dream' to shift until the time is changed, i.e. until that which threatens you is removed. Tell me the dream: and when you have told it I will know that you will be able to tell its interpretation.

The word Mtnmdzh is from the root Nmz, the letter d being servile. He means, You are acting differently than when

24

you used to tell us that you understood secrets.' Nebuchadnezzar must have heard them say that they understood things of this sort. He would not otherwise have demanded it of them, nor would he have killed them except that before this time they had professed such knowledge. Now, however, when his demand had fallen upon them, and they saw no way to meet it, they said time after time, 'Tell us the dream that we may interpret it,' instead of saying 'We are not equal to this.' They simply maintained that he knew the dream and was demanding them to tell him what he remembered, or that he had seen no dream at all, and was demanding of them what he had not seen. This is why he said **false and fraudulent.** When they heard this, they were forced to admit they had lied when they professed that they could reveal secrets.

¹⁰The Chaldeans said in reply to the king, "There is no one on earth who can ᵈ⁻satisfy the king's demand,⁻ᵈ for great king or ruler—none has ever asked such a thing of any magician, exorcist, or Chaldean. ¹¹The thing asked by the king is difficult; there is no one who can tell it to the king except the gods whose abode is not among mortals."ᵉ ¹²Whereupon the king flew into a violent rage, and gave an order to do away with all the wise men of Babylon.

¹³The decree condemning the wise men to death was issued. Daniel and his companions were about to be put to death.

10. None of them addressed the king except *the Chaldees*, who were nearest to him, and spoke for the rest. They said, 'We will tell you the truth. No man can reveal this secret. Don't busy *your* heart *with* any such idea. Don't ask us to do the impossible, imagine that we understand any such thing, or that we are trying to protract the time while your spirit is tormented. So spare us an injustice. Have any of the kings before you ever demanded of his sages what you demand of us?'

11. Appended explanation. **There is no one who can tell**: it is clear to me that they suggested Daniel and his companions as professing such knowledge; then they relegate [the king] to the angels. Hence, in ver. 10 there is no man on the dry land (with reference to the Jewish sages); here, none but the angels know this. 'So be just to us and do not demand of us an impossibility,'

12-13. When he saw that they were honest with him and gave him no hope, he was angry. Therefore, he ordered the slaughter of all those that were present in Babylon. As for the others who were outside Babylon, he ordered them to appear before him, after the slaughter of the sages in

---

ᵈ⁻ *Lit. "flesh."*

⁻ᵈ *Lit. "flesh."*

ᵉ *Meaning uncertain.*

26

Babylon, so he could hear what they had to say. The words, and **they sought Daniel and his comrades**, indicate that they had not been present with the Chaldees during their discussion with the king. This was because they had never professed that they understood mysteries. However, the wise men of Babylon must have said, 'We and others are partners in taking the king's supplies; why should we be killed and not they? Let them be killed too.' And, when the news reached Daniel, he hurried before the king's executioner and learned what had happened from him, then he and went before the king, asked a respite of him, and promised him what he had asked of the wise men.

¹⁴when Daniel remonstrated with Arioch, the captain of the royal guard who had set out to put the wise men of Babylon to death. ¹⁵He spoke up and said to Arioch, the royal officer, "Why is the decree of the king so urgent?" Thereupon Arioch informed Daniel of the matter. ¹⁶So Daniel went to ask the king for time, that he might tell the meaning to the king. ¹⁷Then Daniel went to his house and informed his companions, Hananiah, Mishael, and Azariah, of the matter,

14, 15. Nydx comes from zx like Nydx NmV (Ezra v. 16); hFfcomes from hcf. hpcHhm (it is said) is from the language of the Pharisees, in which the insolent is called xpycH. He tells us that Daniel sought counsel from Arioch, after he had asked him to explain the matter clearly. He took his advice about the question of whether or not he should enter the king's presence and ask him for a respite, or should not go to him for fear of his wrath (lest he might not give him time, but order him slain). Arioch, knowing that the king would give him time and would not deal hastily with him, counseled him to go to the king. Perhaps Arioch asked permission for Daniel, so that he might enter in and ask the king for the respite, and the king answered him favorably. The executioner had been executing the wise men of Babylon one after another; and perhaps had begun with the most honorable.

16. **The meaning**: plainly not without the dream; for the person who did not know the dream could *not* possibly interpret it. He could only interpret when he knew both dream and *interpretation*. Daniel must have promised the king what he had demanded of the wise men, both dream and interpretation; and he did so because it was plain to him, and he was convinced and assured that Almighty God had made him forget the dream in order that He might prove the wise men of Babylon liars in their professions: and reveal the matter to Daniel, so that he could magnify his people who

serve the True God, Who alone shows dreams and reveals secrets.

17. i.e. he told them the cause of the massacre and what he had promised the king.

¹⁸that they might implore the God of Heaven for help regarding this mystery, so that Daniel and his colleagues would not be put to death together with the other wise men of Babylon.
¹⁹The mystery was revealed to Daniel in a night vision; then Daniel blessed the God of Heaven.
²⁰Daniel spoke up and said:

> "Let the name of God be blessed forever and ever,
> For wisdom and power are His.

18. i.e. the four stood crying to God and begging mercy of Him: asking Him to reveal this secret, so they might not be killed with the rest; for they knew that they would not be left while the others were killed, especially after Daniel's promise to the king.

19. As there was no use in revealing the mystery to all four of them, one of them sufficing, He revealed it to Daniel, who was the most eminent of them. Furthermore, the king had not demanded that all the wise men of Babylon show him the dream. If one told him, he would excuse the rest. Do you not see that Daniel said to the executioner, 'Do not destroy the wise men of Babylon?' Next, he tells us that when Almighty God had revealed it to him, he blessed God for that. Evidently, He showed Daniel the dream which the king had seen: i.e. the figure of the image, and the cutting of the stone out of the mountain, and the breaking of the image and the wind carrying away its dust, and how the stone became a mighty mountain.

20 sqq. Observe that he tells us they asked Almighty God to reveal the mystery to them, so they might not be slain like the rest of the wise men of Babylon. He tells us that Daniel thanked Almighty God for having revealed the mystery to him. However, he does not record any thanksgiving by him for their deliverance from death; because to his mind the Glory of God was more important than the deliverance of their souls. Furthermore, if the mystery were revealed, they were without doubt delivered. Then he thanked Almighty

30

God according to what the subject of the dream suggested; **for wisdom and power are His**: as He had furnished him with wisdom which no one else had mastered (cp. v. 23a). Now he ascribed wisdom to Him in one of two senses: either he meant, 'He is the wise and mighty' or he meant, 'He gives wisdom and might to whom He will' (compare for *wisdom* Proverbs 11.6, and for power Deuteronomy 8.18, Isaiah 40.9).

²¹He changes times and seasons,
Removes kings and installs kings;
He gives the wise their wisdom
And knowledge to those who know.
²²He reveals deep and hidden things,
Knows what is in the darkness,
And light dwells with Him.

He changes the times and seasons: *seasons:* i.e. seasons of the year, 'cold, heat, summer, and winter;' *times:* i.e. night and day. No one can do this except the Creator. He **removes kings, and installs kings**, inasmuch as He controls the whole world, He sets up whom He will and removes whom He will. Removes is put before sets up, because kings had been in the world from the beginning, ever since the reign of Nimrod, after the flood (cp. Ecclesiastes. 1.2). He gives wisdom to the wise: with the same meaning as above; wisdom being intellect and discrimination, through which mankind surpasses the animals and each other. We also learn that the wise men and sages of the world are not wise because of the own efforts, but only because God has given them their wisdom and their knowledge. **He reveals deep**: alluding to the unseen world which he compares to an object lying in the deep, so that it cannot be reached; or to something hidden and concealed, so that it is unknown, with the same idea as Isaiah 41.10; or possibly he means, 'He reveals what is in man's heart, which none understand except the Creator of the heart and reins, which are concealed from every one, but known to Him' (Jeremiah 17.10). He **knows what is in the darkness**: which is also hidden from mankind, inasmuch as the eyes cannot see in the dark: whereas the Creator of darkness and light knows what is in the one just as much as He knows what is in the other (Psalms 39.12); the purpose being that He, knowing hidden things, knew what the king had seen, and revealed it to Daniel.

32

²³I acknowledge and praise You,
O God of my fathers,
You who have given me wisdom and power,
For now You have let me know what we asked of You;
You have let us know what concerns the king."

After mentioning these five classes, all corresponding with the matter and circumstances of the dream *(wisdom and strength)* with the amount of both He had bestowed on Daniel, *changing of seasons* with the unpredictable changes undergone by Israel and other nations, shown by the removing of a kingdom and the establishment of a kingdom contained in the dream; and so with the *revealing of secrets,* etc.), he said **O God of my fathers**: referring to the fathers and forefathers whom God had chosen and exalted, Who had dealt so graciously with Daniel because he was of their offspring. He praised God for the wisdom and might which He had given him, which had brought him to his high station before Nebuchadnezzar saw the dream. Now twenty-two years had passed from the time that he had obtained this rank in the king's palace to the present. **For now You made known to us what we asked of You**: referring to the revelation of the king's secret (cp. b). He first described how God had dealt with him from the time of when he stood before the king until the present crisis. Then, he described how God dealt with him in the present situation; and here he associates his companions with himself, in contrast to the previous time, in the words, **what we asked of You**: i.e. I and my companions; similarly **You have made known to us**. He associates his companions with himself, to show that, although the revelation was made to him and not to them, nevertheless it belonged to all of them, since all of them were sought for execution, and all had prayed and humbled themselves (ver. 18). After praising Almighty God for this, he went to Arioch without delay, because he had already pledged his word, and a fixed time had been appointed to him by the king. Possibly he had asked the king for a day and no more; and while they four stood praying, it came to pass that he fell asleep and saw the dream, and woke rejoicing, and told his companions, and they too blessed the Almighty Creator. Possibly he rose in the night, at once, and went to the king to delight him with the news, and to calm the people's horror and anguish. Doubtless the country was dismayed at the massacre of the wise men, and at the thought that the land would be left without them; which is one of the worst misfortunes that can befall a country.

²⁴Thereupon Daniel went to Arioch, whom the king had appointed to do away with the wise men of Babylon; he came and said to him as follows, "Do not do away with the wise men of Babylon; bring me to the king and I will tell the king the meaning!" ²⁵So Arioch rushed Daniel into the king's presence and said to him, "I have found among the exiles of Judah a man who can make the meaning known to the king!" ²⁶The king said in reply to Daniel (who was called Belteshazzar), "Can you really make known to me the dream that I saw and its meaning?"

24. He went to Arioch at once, for two reasons: (1) to stop the massacre; (2) to have Arioch introduce him before the king.

25. The words, **I have found a man**, when the king must have known of Daniel certainly, are plainly a refutation of the words of the wise men: the speaker points out that by the children of the captivity, who were of inferior rank and low esteem among the wise men, behold, this secret will be made known.

26. He had already promised the king that he would tell him the interpretation at the time appointed. The king, though, had no confidence in this. Therefore he said, '*Can you* do this* ?' i.e. 'tell me the dream and its interpretation; let us see what you will say.' He uses, here, the name the chief eunuch gave him, because it was an honorable one.

²⁷Daniel answered the king and said, "The mystery about which the king has inquired—wise men, exorcists, magicians, and diviners cannot tell to the king. ²⁸But there is a God in heaven who reveals mysteries, and He has made known to King Nebuchadnezzar what is to be at the end of days. This is your dream and the vision that entered your mind in bed: ²⁹O king, the thoughts that came to your mind in your bed are about future events; He who reveals mysteries has let you know what is to happen.

27 sqq. By the declaration that neither the wise men of Babylon nor any one else could do what the king had demanded of them, he does not mean to excuse them. His only object is to expose the lies of all the sages of the Gentiles who professed to know mysteries. He will state after this that he too had not learned this secret by himself, but the Creator had revealed it to him. Then he told the king that God Almighty revealed secrets to whom He would, because it was He who showed men dreams; adding that God had made manifest to him (Daniel) the fancies which had entered into Nebuchadnezzar's mind concerning the future.

28. **This is your dream and the vision that entered your mind in bed:** i.e. you have indeed demanded of us what you have seen: and, I will show you what you saw; and you will recognize that I have not added nor taken away from it.

29. He mentions, first, a matter not pertaining to the dream, nor to what the king had forgotten: 'before you slept, or saw the dream, you were thinking of what will happen hereafter to your kingdom, which has reached the summit of its exaltation; and who would receive the kingdom after you. Since this was already in your mind, and you desired to know it, the Revealer of secrets showed you what would come to pass hereafter, so that you would know it and know that the kingdom is to belong to that dynasty which will outlast all dynasties.'

³⁰Not because my wisdom is greater than that of other creatures has this mystery been revealed to me, but in order that the meaning should be made known to the king, and that you may know the thoughts of your mind.
³¹"O king, as you looked on, there appeared a great statue. This statue, which was huge and its brightness surpassing, stood before you, and its appearance was awesome.

30. 'I have not learned this secret through my own wisdom, something unique to me that would put me above the rest of [mankind], as scholars excel one another in different sciences.' The other side [i.e., the power by which he had learned it] he does not explain further than by saying, 'God has revealed this to me so you will know what is to happen, what you were thinking, and that which you wanted to understand.' Now the reason why God showed him the dream was so he would know first, the truth of Israel's assertion that the kingdom is to be given to them and no other nation; and, second, that the kingdom of Nebuchadnezzar will cease and be transferred to another and an inferior, to increase his confusion. Furthermore, it was God's design to show him, also, that the assertion of Israel that God Almighty reveals to them secrets which none beside them understand is true; and that the secret of which his wise men stated, namely that none but the angels could understand it [the secret], had been shown by Almighty God to Daniel. He also wanted to show the king that Almighty God had delivered Daniel and his fellows from death; and that they had delivered the other wise men of Babylon (ver. 24). Doubtless, while he was interpreting the dream, a crowd was present listening to his voice. And at the words *As for you, O King, your thoughts came into your mind upon your bed,* the king said, 'It was so.' That, too, was a mystery revealed to him by God.

31. He attributes four qualities to the image:

(1) *Greatness:* i.e. length, breadth, and height; referring to the length of their duration, and the greatness of their power.

37

(2) *Order* [1]: referring to the good order of their empire(s), and the organization of their kingdom(s).

(3) *Comeliness:* because each one of them had armies.

(4) *Fearfulness and awfulness:* because each dynasty was fearful and terrible, especially to Israel.

---

[1] The words br Nbd are rendered in the translation 'composite.'

³²The head of that statue was of fine gold; its breast and arms were of silver; its belly and thighs, of bronze; ³³its legs were of iron, and its feet part iron and part clay. ³⁴As you looked on, a stone was hewn out, not by hands, and struck the statue on its feet of iron and clay and crushed them. ³⁵All at once, the iron, clay, bronze, silver, and gold were crushed, and became like chaff of the threshing floors of summer; a wind carried them off until no trace of them was left. But the stone that struck the statue became a great mountain and filled the whole earth.

³⁶"Such was the dream, and we will now tell the king its meaning. ³⁷You, O king—king of kings, to whom the God of Heaven has given kingdom, power, might, and glory; ³⁸into whose hands He has given men, wild beasts, and the fowl of heaven, wherever they may dwell; and to whom He has given dominion over them all—you are the head of gold. ³⁹But another kingdom will arise after you, inferior to yours; then yet a third kingdom, of bronze, which will rule over the whole earth. ⁴⁰But the fourth kingdom will be as strong as iron; just as iron crushes and shatters everything—and like iron that smashes—so will it crush and smash all these. ⁴¹You saw the feet and the toes, part potter's clay and part iron; that means it will be a divided kingdom; it will have only some of the stability of iron, inasmuch as you saw iron mixed with common clay. ⁴²And the toes were part iron and part clay; that [means] the kingdom will be in part strong and in part brittle. ⁴³You saw iron mixed with common clay; that means: ^{e-}they shall intermingle with the offspring of men,^{-e} but shall not hold together, just as iron does not mix with clay.

32-35. He tells the king his dream as he had seen it; and the king bore witness to his accuracy. Then he said, 'And now we will interpret it for you:' for none of his wise men could interpret it any more than they could interpret his second dream.

37-43. He notices in the interpretation one of the features of the image, which he had not noticed in the dream. In the

---

^{e-} *Meaning uncertain.*
^{-e} *Meaning uncertain.*

dream, he says, "**its feet part of iron and part clay**," but in the interpretation, "**the feet and the toes**," for a reason which we will explain.

Kingdom, power, might and glory: power, referring to the number of his armies; might, to his vigor; glory, referring to the amount of his wealth and supplies, and the obedience of mankind.

And wherever they may dwell: meaning that all mankind were under his power, so much so that he ruled even the beasts and birds, meaning that he could do with them what he pleased when he assaulted them. Some say there is an allusion to his being with them during the seven years in which he 'abode with them.' This is unlikely; as the words are a description of his present condition, and do not refer to anything in the future. Compare Jeremiah 27.6, referring to the terror which he inspired in the heart of all beasts and birds. Another fancied it referred to the inhabitants of wildernesses and remote islands. Daniel continues: 'And because you have reached this station, and are the first and most splendid of the four kingdoms, you are the fine golden head.' This is the interpretation of the head; 'and he who will rise after you is *inferior to you*,' frx is derived from xfrx 'earth,' and is used metaphorically; meaning, even as the ground is below man's feet. Of this second kingdom he says **another** because its religion and laws were different from those of the Chaldees: he does not explain this, just as he does not dwell on the description of the third kingdom, contenting himself with saying that it is inferior to the silver. **Which will rule over the whole earth**: to distinguish between the second and the third kingdoms. The second kingdom owned three quarters of the world, but the third four quarters. We will give the reader all these explanations in full in the commentary on Daniel's dream. Then he described the fourth kingdom, which he compares to iron, not meaning that it was inferior to the brass, but on account of its hardness (**strong as iron**), and because this kingdom would pulverize armies as iron pulverizes gold, silver, and brass. **Crushes and shatters everything**: i.e. it crushed the kingdoms of its time, as we will explain on ver. 35. This is the kingdom of Rome, before the kingdom of Arabia arose. He makes the head the first kingdom, and the breast and arms the second kingdom, and the belly and thighs the third kingdom: and he makes the upper parts of the legs the fourth kingdom before the kingdom of Arabia. Now he does not say of the fourth kingdom 'another,' as he said of the second and third, because the Greeks are the founders of the kingdom of Rome, as we will show in chap. 8. **You saw the feet and the toes**: feet refers to the instep of the foot; then he mentions the toes, and tells us that the feet and toes of this image were like the feet and toes of a man, two feet and ten toes. Probably, however, the statue resembled a human being also in its erect posture, its back, hips, legs, as well as feet and toes. He unites the feet and toes in the sentence because they were all of the same material, iron and clay (cp. ver. 33). The *iron* represents the Romans, and the *clay* the Arabs. This is because the Romans reigned a hundred years before the Arabs; then the Arabs began to reign, but the kingdom of the Romans remained, as is witnessed in our own day. He compares the kingdom of the Arabs to *clay*, because they have neither power nor force like the Romans. **A divided kingdom**: i.e., from the time of the reign of the Arabs, inasmuch as the kingdom was first the Romans only, then the Arabs reigned with them. And **part iron**: to show that this iron, which is mixed with the clay, is not different from the former iron, but the same. The interpretation is that the kingdom of the Romans will remain simultaneously with the kingdom of the Arabs, and that the Arabs will be partners with them; hence, **part potter's clay**. **Mixed with common**

41

clay: not a mixture in which the ingredients mingle, as gold mixes with silver; as this is not possible between such substances as iron and clay; but a mixture like that of wheat and barley, or similar substances. Part, therefore, of the instep of the foot is iron and part clay. This is possible because of the length of the instep. The same is the case with the toes. In the description of the toes, part of iron and part of clay, probably this iron does not belong to the Romans, but is to be interpreted of the Arabs only. In the interpretation of this he says **so the kingdom will be in part string and in part brittle**. Either he means that its beginnings were powerful (as we will explain in the proper place in this book), and its end feeble (in which case the toes where they joined the instep must have been iron, and the ends clay); or, he may be referring to the kingdom of some of the children of 'the Master' (Mohammed), who were powerful, and others who were to follow them were weak like clay.

Inasmuch as you saw iron mixed with common clay does not refer to the mixture of the toes, since he does not use the word *mixture* of them, but says only **part iron and part clay**. This can only refer to the mixture of the feet, of which he had said **Inasmuch as you saw**, etc. This is the mixture of the Romans and the Arabs. He tells us that just as they are associated in empire (**a divided kingdom**), so they will be mixed in the matter of marrying and begetting children, neither party disapproving of this, as Israel does. For this reason, too, he said **they shall intermingle themselves with the offspring of men**. For the Moslem does not refuse to take a wife of the Christian religion, nor the Christian to take a wife of the religion of Islam.

But they shall not hold together: since they disagree with one another on the fundamental doctrines, the one confessing One God, and believing that 'Isa (Jesus), the son

42

of Maryam (Mary), was a mortal; whereas the others believe that He is the Creator of the heavens and earth, as is well known concerning the Christian religion. Similarly they differ about the Qiblah and many other subjects too long to explain. This is why he says **they shall not hold together;** which is explained in the words **just as iron,** etc., i.e. as iron does not mingle with clay.

So far for the description of the statue, now for the interpretation of it. It means four kingdoms, which are to arise in the world. The first is the kingdom, which laid waste Jerusalem and took the people captive from their homes. *After* it, came the kingdom of the Persians, which ordered the Temple to be built, and permitted the people of Israel to go there, and gave the money, charges and offerings out of its treasures. The *third* is the kingdom of the Greeks, which neither took Israel captive nor laid waste their dwellings: however, harm was done to the nation by them, as the Jews have handed down in their books and records, though the books of the Prophets do not expressly state it. As for the *fourth* empire, it has carried Israel into captivity, as the first did, and gone further than it in enmity and injury. As for the Arabs, they have not acted like the others in exiling them and destroying them, but they have injured the nation in the way of contempt, scorn and humiliation, etc., of which we will mention some specimens in the commentary on the dream of Daniel and his prophecy. He represents all these empires as attached to each other, because there was not a follower of the truth among them, though their systems differed: and he makes them all one piece.

After giving the interpretation of the image he gives that of the stone, which was cut from the mountain and broke the image.

⁴⁴And in the time of those kings, the God of Heaven will establish a kingdom that shall never be destroyed, a kingdom that shall not be transferred to another people. It will crush and wipe out all these kingdoms, but shall itself last forever—⁴⁵just as you saw how a stone was hewn from the mountain, not by hands, and crushed the iron, bronze, clay, silver, and gold. The great God has made known to the king what will happen in the future. The dream is sure and its interpretation reliable."

44, 45. He compared the four kingdoms to a wrought image, but the kingdom of Israel to a stone cut out of a mountain, because their kingdom is eternal: either it means the *nation*, or the *Messiah*, who is of them, or of the seed of David. He said in the dream that it *broke the feet of the image*, i.e. that they will crush Edom (i.e., Rome) and Ishmael. Then he says **they were broken in pieces together**, inasmuch as the religion of each kingdom and some, too, of the people will remain until the Messiah's kingdom. He tells us that it will break and destroy the remnants of the three previous kingdoms, their religions; **it will break in pieces and consume all these kingdoms.** He points out the difference between these four kingdoms and that of the Messiah. Of every one of these four kingdoms the dominion ceases, and is given to another. However, this kingdom will not pass away, nor be given to another. He did not say of the image that God Almighty had set it up, as he says of the kingdom of the Messiah, **"the God of heaven will establish a kingdom,"** because they are weak and few in number. It is God who will raise them from the dust, and bring down the others from the height, since it was he who brought them down from the height (Lamentations 11.12) and raised the empire of the others (*ibid.* 11.14). He will do the same in the time to come, raising Israel and afflicting the empires (cp. Psalms 63.5). God Almighty showed this dream to Nebuchadnezzar, because he was the first of the kings and the greatest of them.

44

God wanted to show him, and every king who would arise, the superiority of Israel, what would come to pass in the latter days, that every dynasty would be destroyed when her empire began, and that none should think itself a lasting dynasty. He wanted to show that it will be well for these dynasties not to afflict Israel, because they are suffering discipline, that is all. If they do otherwise, God will be angry with them and punish them. Thereby, He teaches His people to be patient, knowing the vicissitudes of these empires and the durability of their own, and that all nations will bow before them. Therein is their great consolation.

The dream is sure, and its interpretation reliable: i.e. this dream did not come from fancy, or mental preoccupation. Men sometimes see in dreams what they have been doing or thinking of, and when they see it, there is no interpretation to be realized in the future. However, this was a dream that God purposefully showed him.

And its interpretation reliable: i.e. this interpretation of mine is accurate, and there is no explanation other than what we have given.

⁴⁶Then King Nebuchadnezzar prostrated himself and paid homage to Daniel and ordered that a meal offering and pleasing offerings be made to him. ⁴⁷The king said in reply to Daniel, "Truly your God must be the God of gods and Lord of kings and the revealer of mysteries to have enabled you to reveal this mystery." ⁴⁸The king then elevated Daniel and gave him very many gifts, and made him governor of the whole province of Babylon and chief prefect of all the wise men of Babylon. ⁴⁹At Daniel's request, the king appointed Shadrach, Meshach, and Abed-nego to administer the province of Babylon; while Daniel himself was at the king's court.

46. Believing that there was in Daniel a portion of divine power, like what the Christians hold of the Messiah, he put him in the place of God, and fell on his face before him and bowed down to him. He commanded that sacrifices be brought to him, as they are brought to a god. He does not say that he *brought* them to him: most probably Daniel prohibited him from doing so.

47. **Truly**: he acknowledges that God is the God of gods, and that it was through Him that Daniel could know this mystery. Then he called him Master[1] (i.e., made himself his pupil and his slave). Then he bestowed on him many splendid gifts, as he had promised the Chaldees, ver. 6; adding a distinction which he had not expressly mentioned to them, viz. making him Sultan of the province of Babylon and chief of all the wise men of Babylon.

49. When he had attained high station it was impossible for him that his companions should be left with no station. As for himself, he was established in the king's gate - not as porter, but rather to inspect men's business in the same way Joseph did: The king had the title and Daniel gave the commands and prohibitions. The writer tells us of the rank of his associates by way of introduction to the sequel.

---

[1] Translation of ver. 48: 'Then the king called Daniel my lord, and my master,' etc.

46

King Nebuchadnezzar made a statue of gold sixty cubits high and six cubits broad. He set it up in the plain of Dura in the province of Babylon. [2]King Nebuchadnezzar then sent word to gather the satraps, prefects, governors, counselors, treasurers, judges, officers, and all the provincial officials to attend the dedication of the statue that King Nebuchadnezzar had set up. [3]So the satraps, prefects, governors, counselors, treasurers, judges, officers, and all the provincial officials assembled for the dedication of the statue that King Nebuchadnezzar had set up, and stood before the statue that Nebuchadnezzar had set up. [4]The herald proclaimed in a loud voice, "You are commanded, O peoples and nations of every language, [5]when you hear the sound of the horn, pipe, zither, lyre, psaltery, bagpipe, and all other types of instruments, to fall down and worship the statue of gold that King Nebuchadnezzar has set up. [6]Whoever will not fall down and worship shall at once be thrown into a burning fiery furnace." [7]And so, as soon as all the peoples heard the sound of the horn, pipe, zither, lyre, psaltery, and all other types of instruments, all peoples and nations of every language fell down and worshiped the statue of gold that King Nebuchadnezzar had set up. [8]Seizing the occasion, certain Chaldeans came forward to slander the Jews. [9]They spoke up and said to King Nebuchadnezzar, "O king, live forever! [10]You, O king, gave an order that everyone who hears the horn, pipe, zither, lyre, psaltery, bagpipe, and all types of instruments must fall down and worship the golden statue, [11]and whoever does not fall down and worship shall be thrown into a burning fiery furnace.

III.

The matter narrated here belongs to the history of Nebuchadnezzar, but Hananiah, Mishael, and Azaria enter into it. It is told us on account of the great enlightenment to be obtained from it. The first thing necessary to explain is, "What moved Nebuchadnezzar to make this image?" Our answer is, that he made it when he became master of the

47

world; and the herald proclaimed that whoever would not come forward and bow down to the image would be cast into the fiery furnace. By doing this they would show their allegiance to him. Before they were under his sovereignty he could not have done it. He already had another deity whom he served (ver. 14). His will was accomplished as soon as it was seen that all mankind - except the Jews mentioned in the Scripture - bowed down to it. He records its *height* and its *size;* the latter containing its length and breadth. He set it up in the plain of Dūra because it could contain a great crowd of men standing. He made its *height sixty cubits,* so that they could see it from a distance and bow down to it from every quarter. He did not set it up before collecting the people: rather, he made it first, then sent and brought the people from all the cities of the world. When they had come to Babylon he set it up and ordered them to bow down to it. He brought the nobles, not the common people, which would have been impossible. The world would have been desolated and the place could not have contained them either. Those who came must have left substitutes to keep their places until they returned. He tells us that when they were summoned *they came* and did not disobey. This fact, by itself, showed their allegiance to him. And when they were gathered in Babylon, he made a banquet in honor of the image; and the people gathered and bowed down, and after that went to eat and drink. They did not eat before they had bowed. Probably he had slaughtered sacrifices and made them ready for the people. Then, after they had gathered together, he set up musicians with their instruments. When they were standing in front of the image, he commanded the heralds to go among the people and say: 'Take heed, and do not fail to bow down to the image. Whenever you hear the sound of the musical instruments, let every one fall on his face bowing to the image. Whoever will not bow down, that moment will

48

he be cast into the fiery furnace.' This shows that he must have built a great furnace in order that if any man disobeyed he might be thrown into the fire. Most probably he had sent some people before him to go about among the people who had come from the countries, to see whether any one disobeyed or not. Then the writer informs us that all who were present bowed down after they had heard the sound of the musical instruments, except the three mentioned above. We are left with one of two alternatives, either he desired the people to abandon their religions and serve a god other than their own; or he desired their allegiance only. As it is not probable that he desired them to give up their gods, since the religions remained intact, each nation serving its god, we must suppose that he desired their allegiance and nothing more. What we must remember about all the Jews who were in Babylon is that the king did not require this of the common people, but only of the dignitaries and nobles: not of the others. Had not Hananiah, Mishael, and Azaria been dignitaries - as was mentioned before - he would not have made them appear in the crowd, nor have required them to bow down. As for the case of Daniel, he was not required to bow down to the image because his station was too high: he occupied the place of a god with the king (11.46). Those who accused them were servants of the king, whom he had ordered to take note of the people.

¹²There are certain Jews whom you appointed to administer the province of Babylon, Shadrach, Meshach, and Abed-nego; those men pay no heed to you, O king; they do not serve your god or worship the statue of gold that you have set up."

¹³Then Nebuchadnezzar, in raging fury, ordered Shadrach, Meshach, and Abed-nego to be brought; so those men were brought before the king. ¹⁴Nebuchadnezzar spoke to them and said, "Is it true, Shadrach, Meshach, and Abed-nego, that you do not serve my god or worship the statue of gold that I have set up? ¹⁵Now if you are ready to fall down and worship the statue that I have made when you hear the sound of the horn, pipe, zither, lyre, psaltery, and bagpipe, and all other types of instruments, [well and good]; but if you will not worship, you shall at once be thrown into a burning fiery furnace, and what god is there that can save you from my power?"

12. **They do not serve your god**: i.e. the god whom he served before he set up the image.

We learn that when he was told that they *did not bow down to the image*, **he was filled with wrath and his color changed.** Either this was because [text fragmented]   or because opposition had come from *them* [and he feared] that, when this was known to others, his authority would be weakened.   Had it not been for that, he would not have thought it a serious matter. The latter is more probable to my mind. He did not know what to do, and perhaps did not finish the dedication of the image.

He ordered them to be brought before him and began to reproach them.   Perhaps, he thought, they would make an excuse of some kind, so that their joy would not be troubled (i.e., so that they could avoid punishment).

15. **Now are you ready?** i.e., 'did you just now hear the proclamation, or has the herald not yet come forward with it?' Perhaps he said this in order that they might make some excuse, that the people might know they did not slight him. Though the time for bowing had already passed.   For he only desired the people to bow down at the time when they heard

the sound of the musical instruments. The answer they returned, however, was not an excuse. On the contrary, they spoke plainly to him, so that it became necessary, in his view, for him to do what he did.

¹⁶Shadrach, Meshach, and Abed-nego said in reply to the king, "O Nebuchadnezzar, we have no need to answer you in this matter, ¹⁷for if so it must be, our God whom we serve is able to save us from the burning fiery furnace, and He will save us from your power, O king. ¹⁸But even if He does not, be it known to you, O king, that we will not serve your god or worship the statue of gold that you have set up."

¹⁹Nebuchadnezzar was so filled with rage at Shadrach, Meshach, and Abed-nego that his visage was distorted, and he gave an order to heat up the furnace to seven times its usual heat. ²⁰He commanded some of the strongest men of his army to bind Shadrach, Meshach, and Abed-nego, and to throw them into the burning fiery furnace. ²¹So these men, in their shirts, trousers, hats, and other garments, were bound and thrown into the burning fiery furnace.

16. **We have no need**: i.e. 'it is not necessary for us to make any excuse, as perhaps you would suggest. As for your saying, **"What god is he,"** you should know that our God is able to deliver us from the fiery furnace you threaten us with in many ways. If you command us to be killed by some other means, He is able to deliver us from that too.'

18. **But even if He does not**: this does not mean 'if He is not able,' which would be in contradiction to their assertion, ver. 17. It means, 'if He should not deliver us. For He will not leave us in your hand out of His inability to save us. Nor do we serve Him in order that He may deliver us from punishment in this world, but only that we may be delivered from punishment in the next world, and receive our eternal reward. So you may know that what was told you of us is true; we have not served your god, nor your image nor will we serve them in time to come either.' This they said in the presence of the crowds that had bowed down to the image.

From this verse we learn that it is unlawful to bow down to an image, even though a man does not believe in its sanctity. The foundation of this is in the law (Exodus 20.5).

We also learn that there is another world of rewards. For, if there were no other world after this, in what did they trust, that they did not bow down to the image? In what did they hope, that they gave their bodies to be burnt? Or why did Daniel let himself be thrown into the lions' den? The words "if... not" show that in their opinion it was possible that God might let His servants be tormented and slain by the hand of unbelievers, to reward them for it in the next world. They knew all this, and yet did not commit the crime of bowing down to the image.

He ordered them to throw in **seven times** as much wood as was ordinarily thrown in, to terrify them, so they might repent and humble themselves. For their part, they did not care for his words or think about them. Then we are told that he commanded them to be bound **in their clothes**; and the king's order was obeyed.

NVhywyFp their vests.

NVhtLbrk their belts.

NVhywVbL, either their turbans, or their bonnets, as they were dressed like governors.

They were *thrown* with machines, because the furnace was high, and raised above the level of the ground, and they were thrown over the top of it. They were not put in by the door of the furnace, because the king wished to make the scene as terrible as possible, in order that the crowds of bystanders might look on at a distance, on some high ground. Possibly he flung in each one separately, one after the other. He threw in, let us suppose, Hananiah first, that the two might become frightened. Nevertheless, they did not care; so he threw in the second, and the last did not care either.

²²Because the king's order was urgent, and the furnace was heated to excess, a tongue of flame killed the men who carried up Shadrach, Meshach, and Abed-nego. ²³But those three men, Shadrach, Meshach, and Abed-nego, dropped, bound, into the burning fiery furnace.

²⁴Then King Nebuchadnezzar was astonished and, rising in haste, addressed his companions, saying, "Did we not throw three men, bound, into the fire?" They spoke in reply, "Surely, O king." ²⁵He answered, "But I see four men walking about unbound and unharmed in the fire and the fourth looks like a divine being." ²⁶Nebuchadnezzar then approached the hatch of the burning fiery furnace and called, "Shadrach, Meshach, Abed-nego, servants of the Most High God, come out!" So Shadrach, Meshach, and Abed-nego came out of the fire. ²⁷The satraps, the prefects, the governors, and the royal companions gathered around to look at those men, on whose bodies the fire had had no effect, the hair of whose heads had not been singed, whose shirts looked no different, to whom not even the odor of fire clung.

22. The writer now tells us how those who threw them in were killed by the heat of the sparks of fire. This was because the fuel flew up when they fell in, and a fierce flame came out of it. When the heat caught them, they perished. Nebuchadnezzar was standing on the high place when they flung them out of the machine, looking on the furnace. There can have been no smoke ascending, which would have hidden the furnace from view. He saw them, and behold, they were going back and forth in the flame. He was terrified and amazed by what he saw (ver. 24), and spoke to his courtiers as recorded. Either these were present with him, but did not see what he saw (God hiding it from them as happened to Daniel when he saw the angel whom no one else saw, as we will explain *infra),* so that they saw neither the angel nor the three. Or it may be that his courtiers saw the three, but did not see the angel.

24. **Did we not throw three men?** He tells them that he

sees something they do not. Perhaps he asked first for information from them, to know whether they saw it or not; and then he said 'Didn't we throw in three men and no more?' They responded 'Yes.' Then he said, 'I see four people, only the fourth is like the angels.' The other three were, of course, Shadrach, etc. Then, when he saw them going back and forth in the furnace, not going out of it, he said to himself, 'These men will not go out, however long they stay. It is as if they were in a garden, relaxing.' So he approached the door of the furnace to ask them to come out from it, since there was no way out except by the door. Apparently they wanted to show the crowd that the king must command them to exit the furnace. They would not go out except by his command. So he approached the furnace and said to them, 'Come out, come.' The angel must have been with them until they left the furnace, because so long as he was with them no damage from the fire could come to them. When they went out, they were not naked, but clothed; in their tunics only, out of all their clothes, since only these are mentioned. The Creator and Worker of miracles caused these tunics to remain, to cover them, so all who were present could see the miracle that some of their clothes should be burnt, while others remained unburned. We are told above that the fire did not attack any part of their *bodies*, so that even in the nails of their feet and hands, in which no great harm would be done, they were not injured. **Their hair was not singed**: as hair is naturally by a little fire when it comes near it. **To whom not even the odor of fire clung**. on them: it could not be smelt in their bodies or in their tunics. This is not astonishing, as a work of the Almighty Creator. He put a screen between the fire and them, through one of those mercies of which he is capable but not between the fire and their garments; blessed be He, Worker of miracles impossible to His creatures (cp. Psalms 136.4). This disproves the

55

doctrine of those who would discount miracles, and. reject this narrative. Now God Almighty displayed this mighty miracle in the time of Nebuchadnezzar, as He displayed His miracles in Egypt, annulling the works of the Magicians until they confessed and said, 'This is the finger of God' (Exodus 7.15). And so, when Nebuchadnezzar and the rest of his princes had witnessed this, they believed, in the work of the Creator. Thereafter, he blessed the Creator, saying: Blessed is their God, etc., An hour before his language to them had been: **and who is the God who will save you from my hand?**

²⁸Nebuchadnezzar spoke up and said, "Blessed be the God of Shadrach, Meshach, and Abed-nego, who sent His angel to save His servants who, trusting in Him, flouted the king's decree at the risk of their lives rather than serve or worship any god but their own God. ²⁹I hereby give an order that [anyone of] any people or nation of whatever language who blasphemes the God of Shadrach, Meshach, and Abed-nego shall be torn limb from limb, and his house confiscated, for there is no other God who is able to save in this way."

³⁰Thereupon the king promoted Shadrach, Meshach, and Abed-nego in the province of Babylon.

Who sent His angel: he had witnessed the angel going with them; God Almighty had sent the angel to make him certain that this was His work, and none other's. **To save His servants:** observing that they were saved through relying on Him, not caring for his threats, and changing the king's word. **But gave up their bodies:** i.e. they gave over their bodies to the fire, rather than serve another god.

I hereby give an order: he ordered that a stop be put to the societies of religious speculation, where the doctrines of the monotheists were corrupted. **That whoever spoke error against their God will be cut into pieces,** i.e. his body cut in pieces, and his property be confiscate to the sultan.

For there is no other God: he decides that among all the gods there is none able to deliver his servants from distress and punishments like Him.

After this he tells us what the king did with them afterwards. He promoted, i.e., he increased their rank and dignity.

People may ask about the previous assertion of Nebuchadnezzar at the time when Daniel interpreted his dream for him, 'Of a truth your God, etc.,' and they may say, 'Does not this language show that he believed in God Almighty and His miracles? How then can he have dealt so with Shadrach, etc., or said, "And who is the God who will

57

save you from my hand?'" The answer is that it was not more extraordinary than that our ancestors should have witnessed God's wonders and His talking with them on Mount Sinai, and a few days later serve the golden calf, explaining away in some manner what they had witnessed. How much more natural that this would be the conduct of Nebuchadnezzar the idolater! At the time, probably, he believed. Afterwards, he apostatized because some of these false explanations. Doubtless, God punished him for his apostasy, and for admitting doubts into his mind.

³¹"King Nebuchadnezzar to all people and nations of every language that inhabit the whole earth: May your well-being abound! ³²The signs and wonders that the Most High God has worked for me I am pleased to relate. ³³How great are His signs; how mighty His wonders! His kingdom is an everlasting kingdom, and His dominion endures throughout the generations."

31. These are the letters written by king Nebuchadnezzar to all the people of the world, after the completion of the seven years which passed over him when he was among the wild beasts. When his reason had returned to him and he was once more king, he wrote the letters, in which he narrates the story; beginning with **Signs and wonders**, and ending with **and those that walk in pride**.

32. **Signs and wonders**: alluding to what had happened to him during the seven years, which we will recount in its place. It was pleasing before me: meaning that he felt bound to tell them to the world, and not to refrain from publishing and proclaiming them, and thanking God for them.

33. **His signs**: i.e. both the wonderful works recorded above, and those, which God is constantly performing. Showing that he believed in them, and did not reject them as the philosophers do.

His kingdom is an everlasting kingdom: meaning (1) that it endures infinitely; (2) that He does what He thinks fit in His world, and that His dominion is over all while the times and periods change (cp. Psalms 145. 13).

I, Nebuchadnezzar, was living serenely in my house, flourishing in my palace. [2]I had a dream that frightened me, and my thoughts in bed and the vision of my mind alarmed me. [3]I gave an order to bring all the wise men of Babylon before me to let me know the meaning of the dream. [4]The magicians, exorcists, Chaldeans, and diviners came, and I related the dream to them, but they could not make its meaning known to me.

IV.

1. He tells us that he saw the dream at the time when he was at peace: the world being completely at his feet, without enemies or rivals; his affairs and business being all in order.

flourishing in my palace refers to his bodily health and personal appearance when his affairs were settled, as opposed to the condition in which he was during the periods when he was engaged in wars.

2. He tells us that he saw a dream which made an impression on him, and which he did not forget as he had forgotten the first dream: and when he woke, he was in terror. Or, the first part may be a description of his condition during the time in which he was seeing the dream and hearing the voice of the angels, **Cut down the oak**; and the words **and thoughts in bed and the vision of my mind alarmed me**, an account of his condition after waking, meaning that he was reflecting on what he had seen, and troubled and amazed, not knowing the interpretation.

3, 4. He did not, we see, send for Daniel to appear before him, and ask him to interpret the dream, notwithstanding that Daniel was present in Babylon. He sent first to the wise men of Babylon for the following reason: when he demanded of them the first dream, they said repeatedly, 'Tell us the dream and we undertake to interpret it.' So when he saw this dream, knowing that its interpretation was difficult, he decided to tell it to the different orders of wise men of Babylon. He did this so that, when they were found unable to interpret it, their inferiority might be clearly proved to them and to mankind in general. Afterwards he would send for Daniel, who would tell him the dream before them, and explain it step by step. Therefore, his superiority would come out as clearly as that of Joseph, when the wise men of Egypt were unable to interpret the dream of Pharaoh, and they all acknowledged his wisdom (Genesis 41.38).

⁵Finally, Daniel, called Belteshazzar after the name of my god, in whom the spirit of the holy gods was, came to me, and I related the dream to him, [saying], ⁶"Belteshazzar, chief magician, in whom I know the spirit of the holy gods to be, and whom no mystery baffles, tell me the meaning of my dream vision that I have seen. ⁷In the visions of my mind in bed

I saw a tree of great height in the midst of the earth;
⁸The tree grew and became mighty;
Its top reached heaven,
⁹And it was visible to the ends of the earth.
Its foliage was beautiful
And its fruit abundant;
There was food for all in it.
Beneath it the beasts of the field found shade,
And the birds of the sky dwelt on its branches;
All creatures fed on it.

¹⁰In the vision of my mind in bed, I looked and saw a holy Watcher coming down from heaven.

5, 6. He had called him **Belteshazzar, the name of his god**, because of the **spirit of the holy gods** which was to be found in him; the name was a distinction.

According to the name of my god: some have supposed that in spite of all the events which had happened to him, he continued to worship idols, owing to some delusion or other, or else for political purposes. This was as if he proclaimed to the world that he adopted the religion of the Jews, their laws would be incumbent on him, and he would fall. He was therefore unwilling to withdraw himself from his god, so that he magnified the God of heaven, but did not give up his own religion. Or it may refer to that which he had been accustomed to serve before he believed in God Almighty.

Whom I know, from what had occurred in the first dream, when the secret had been revealed to him.

7 sqq. After being told the dream, and how 'none but the of the wise men of Babylon can interpret it, but you can

because of the divine wisdom that is in you, so tell its interpretation,' Daniel thought and did not begin interpreting until the king spoke to him. This was not bewilderment on Daniel's part regarding the interpretation, because the matter was concealed from him. He was rather, pondering how to approach the king, it being improper to approach him directly with the interpretation, because of its content, viz., misfortunes to happen to him. He also saw that it would not be well with him if, when the king asked him for the interpretation, he were to fail to give it. He thought it therefore the safest course to contemplate until the king spoke and asked him. The severe effort of thinking had made his color change. When the king saw him thus he said, 'Don't let the dream or its interpretation trouble you,' thinking that he would need to think deeply over it. Daniel answered that he had not held back the interpretation because it had troubled him, but only on the king's behalf; otherwise he might have rushed to interpret it at once.

[11]He called loudly and said:
'Hew down the tree, lop off its branches,
Strip off its foliage, scatter its fruit.
Let the beasts of the field flee from beneath it
And the birds from its branches,
[12]But leave the stump with its roots in the ground.
In fetters of iron and bronze
In the grass of the field,
Let him be drenched with the dew of heaven,
And share earth's verdure with the beasts.
[13]Let his mind be altered from that of a man,
And let him be given the mind of a beast,
And let seven seasons pass over him.
[14]This sentence is decreed by the Watchers;
This verdict is commanded by the Holy Ones
So that all creatures may know
That the Most High is sovereign over the realm of man,
And He gives it to whom He wishes
And He may set over it even the lowest of men.'
    [15]"I, King Nebuchadnezzar, had this dream; now you,
Belteshazzar, tell me its meaning, since all the wise men of my
kingdom are not able to make its meaning known to me, but you
are able, for the spirit of the holy gods is in you."
    [16]Then Daniel, called Belteshazzar, was perplexed for a
while, and alarmed by his thoughts. The king addressed him,
"Let the dream and its meaning not alarm you." Belteshazzar
replied, "My lord, would that the dream were for your enemy and
its meaning for your foe! [17]The tree that you saw grow and
become mighty, whose top reached heaven, which was visible
throughout the earth,[18]whose foliage was beautiful, whose fruit
was so abundant that there was food for all in it, beneath which
the beasts of the field dwelt, and in whose branches the birds of
the sky lodged—

    16. **Would that the dream were for your enemy**: an
expression of civility and courtesy; it would be improper to
commence otherwise. It has been thought that Daniel may
have meant the *enemies* of God Almighty, and *those that hate
Him* - Nebuchadnezzar being one of them. Then he divided

64

the dream into three parts, and interpreted each part separately.

¹⁹it is you, O king, you who have grown and become mighty, whose greatness has grown to reach heaven, and whose dominion is to the end of the earth. ²⁰The holy Watcher whom the king saw descend from heaven and say,

> Hew down the tree and destroy it,
> But leave the stump with its roots in the ground.
> In fetters of iron and bronze
> In the grass of the field,
> Let him be drenched with the dew of heaven,
> And share the lot of the beasts of the field
> Until seven seasons pass over him—

20. 'The greatness, might and height of the tree that you saw, with food there for all animals, and dwelling for them beneath it and in it,' represents the height of the kingdom and its extension to the end of the world. One thing is left unexplained, sc. v. 21: **Whose leaves and fruit were fair**; the first refers to the beauty of his armies and his children, and the second to the quantity of goods that he had collected from the countries. **In it was food for all** refers to his stores. The beasts of the field had shadow under it: i.e. the nomads. The birds symbolize all those who had come to him from all countries, attached themselves to His dominion and housed themselves under his protection. **And all flesh was fed from it** most probably refers to the profit enjoyed by mankind after his dominion had been established. Then he expounds the second part, the voice of the angels, which he had heard (ver. 14). Observe that of these two angels one was in the height - the one that said Hew down the tree, who is called a watcher - and was higher in rank than the holy one who asked the watcher to let the roots of the tree remain in their place (ver. 15). The sentence is by the decree of the watchers, refers to Hew down the tree, etc. The demand is by the word of the holy one that the stump of his roots should be left. The names are used first in the singular (ver. 13): afterwards in the plural (ver. 17). This shows that they were a multitude; and

that a number of watchers commanded, and a number of holy ones asked on behalf of the tree: God showed him this so he would know that both matters were by command of the Almighty Creator; both Nebuchadnezzar's personal calamity, and the preservation of the kingdom for him until he returned from the wilderness.

Cut down the oak: means removing him from mankind

cut off its branches: refers to the cutting off of his armies. Even with a hand of iron and brass refers to his being among the animals during that period, like a man bound, unable to move here or there, and remaining with the wild beasts. In the tender grass of the field means that he would live in a place which produced grass for him to feed upon, and that he would be a graminivorous not a carnivorous animal.

With the dew of heaven refers to his being day and night under heaven, having no shelter to take refuge in from the dew.

Let his heart be changed refers to the cessation of his reason, and his becoming deprived of the power of discrimination which he had.

Three things, it is to be observed, are literal: (1) grass like an ox, etc.; (2) let it be wet with the dew of heaven; (3) let his heart be changed; the rest are all symbolic.

And let seven times pass over him: some people have thought these times mean 'seasons,' making a total of less than two years; others, that they were years, which is more probable. The period apparently was extended, and the Creator humiliated him. Then the angel states that all this had come upon him so he would know that the kingdom is God's, and that He gives it to whomever He chooses - though he is the lowest of the people (ver. 17). This shows that his heart was swollen, and he had become prideful. God humbled him in consequence, so he would realize that God

Almighty is Monarch in His world; and He does there what He will, as is explained in the following chapter. Then he proceeds to the third portion, and whereas they commanded, you have heard it said 'leave the stump of the roots of the tree;' the meaning of this is that the kingdom remains for you and will not be taken away from you. Then, after he had interpreted the dream, he proceeded to counsel him, he only had to follow this to avert the threat.

²¹this is its meaning, O king; it is the decree of the Most High which has overtaken my lord the king. ²²You will be driven away from men and have your habitation with the beasts of the field. You will be fed grass like cattle, and be drenched with the dew of heaven; seven seasons will pass over you until you come to know that the Most High is sovereign over the realm of man, and He gives it to whom He wishes. ²³And the meaning of the command to leave the stump of the tree with its roots is that the kingdom will remain yours from the time you come to know that Heaven is sovereign. ²⁴Therefore, O king, may my advice be acceptable to you: Redeem your sins by beneficence and your iniquities by generosity to the poor; then your serenity may be extended."
²⁵All this befell King Nebuchadnezzar.

24. This points to his having tyrannized over the people (cp. Ezekiel 7.11; Jeremiah 21.35). He may have made heavy demands from them or enacted cruel laws. The words **generosity to the poor** refer to hard-heartedness on his part towards *the weak*. Some have thought that the *weak* Israelite nation is intended, since apparently he was more furious against them than any others. Now these are two great offences committed by unbelievers for which God punishes in this world. Therefore, he destroyed the generation of the Flood on their account (Genesis 6.13), and so too Sodom and Gomorrah, and so too the people of Nineveh until they repented (Jonah 3.8).

Then your serenity may be extended: i.e. God will divert it from you for a time, as he diverted the disaster in the time of Hezekiah. God would bring it upon him because of his oppression and tyranny: However, if he mended his ways, God would divert it from him. It will be according to the sentence of the watchers, if you remain in all your sins.

25. This verse is not part of Daniel's address to the king, but an observation of the writer, informing us that Nebuchadnezzar did not accept Daniel's counsel, and therefore that which the dream symbolized overtook him.

69

²⁶Twelve months later, as he was walking on the roof of the royal palace at Babylon, ²⁷the king exclaimed, "There is great Babylon, which I have built by my vast power to be a royal residence for the glory of my majesty!" ²⁸The words were still on the king's lips, when a voice fell from heaven, "It has been decreed for you, O King Nebuchadnezzar: The kingdom has passed out of your hands. ²⁹You are being driven away from men, and your habitation is to be with the beasts of the field. You are to be fed grass like cattle, and seven seasons will pass over you until you come to know that the Most High is sovereign over the realm of man and He gives it to whom He wishes." ³⁰There and then the sentence was carried out upon Nebuchadnezzar. He was driven away from men, he ate grass like cattle, and his body was drenched with the dew of heaven until his hair grew like eagle's [feathers] and his nails like [the talons of] birds.

26, 27. This saying was not the only cause of what happened to him, but his continuance in his guilt and transgression. God gave him a year's grace from the time that he saw the dream. Nevertheless, as he did not repent, and this saying was given as a warning, God delayed his punishment no longer. It happened that he had gone up to the roof of the palace, looked down over the city, and observed the beauty of its buildings, until he said **Is not this great Babylon?** which shows that he had rebuilt it after his own fancy to make it his capital; and all his stores were there, hence the words **for the might of my power,** etc.

28, 29. The voice that he heard was from heaven. Possibly no one heard it except he; or possibly others did hear it, the voice being audible that mankind in general might know this.

30. Doubtless, as soon as he heard this voice which descended from the heavens, his reason stopped, he fell down from his palace-roof, went blindly forward, and was guided by the Creator into the wilderness. He was not stopped, especially as his story was known, and Daniel had

told them about it, so that they did not attend to him.

Until his hair grew points to the length of his sojourn, which was seven years.

³¹"When the time had passed, I, Nebuchadnezzar, lifted my eyes to heaven, and my reason was restored to me. I blessed the Most High, and praised and glorified the Ever-Living One,
Whose dominion is an everlasting dominion
And whose kingdom endures throughout the generations.
³²All the inhabitants of the earth are of no account.
He does as He wishes with the host of heaven,
And with the inhabitants of the earth.
There is none to stay His hand
Or say to Him, 'What have You done?'

31, 32. At the end of the seven times his reason returned to him, he found himself among the wild beasts in the wilderness - perceived the state of his body, the mass of his hair and the length of his nails - and realized that all that had been told him had happened to him. After that he raised his eyes to heaven and spoke as above.

His kingdom is an everlasting kingdom, inasmuch as the kingdom of men and their dominion ceases and terminates.

And all the inhabitants of the earth; the great and the little alike are counted as nothing; since they come to an end and die. In this sense, the verse will refer to ordinary people, and their general condition. The prophets and saints however are the pillars of the world. If Nebuchadnezzar refers to death and the termination of man's career, then it is a general sentiment; but if it refers to rank and power, then the prophets and saints are not included.

And he does as he whishes with the host of heaven: i.e. either the angels; or the stars, which eclipse, blacken, and fall.

And with the inhabitants of the earth: here too he may refer to mankind - whom God slays and makes alive, enriches and makes poor - or it may include all the animals.

There is none: including the host of heaven and the inhabitants of the earth.

to stay His hand: i.e. upon God's hand; or perhaps on his own hand, to warn Him off. The first is more probable. None among the host of heaven and the inhabitants of the earth can keep Him from His will, or express displeasure at His work, saying to Him, 'What is the work that You have done? It is not fair' (cp. Ecclesiastes 8.4) - He notices this because it corresponds with his own case; since he had been unable to impede God's dealings with himself, or be displeased thereat, for He had been just in His work. Daniel had warned him, but he had not listened. Therefore, he earned all that happened to him.

³³There and then my reason was restored to me, and my majesty and splendor were restored to me for the glory of my kingdom. My companions and nobles sought me out, and I was reestablished over my kingdom, and added greatness was given me. ³⁴So now I, Nebuchadnezzar, praise, exalt, and glorify the King of Heaven, all of whose works are just and whose ways are right, and who is able to humble those who behave arrogantly."

33. He said above (ver. 31) **my reason was restored to me** in order to annex to it **and I blessed the most High.** Here he repeats it to tell us how he returned and was established in his sovereignty and glory. Daniel had said to him **your kingdom will be sure to you,** assuring him that he would certainly return to his throne.

My companions and nobles sought me out: Daniel had calculated the times, and when they were full, he commanded the army and the nobles to go out after him, and disperse in different regions to seek him, until they found him seeking the inhabited world, and took him and brought him back.

And added greatness: he was not humiliated in their eyes when the disaster had fallen upon him. On the contrary, they gave him increased might and majesty. This was because he dealt justly with the people, and gave up oppression, wrong, and tyranny. Fear of him was in consequence put into the hearts of men, and he increased in power and glory. The Scripture does not tell us how the world fared during these seven times without a king to govern. Some say Daniel governed the kingdom; others that the king's son Evil sat on the throne until the return of his father.

34. Just as if he had been reading out to them this section from the beginning until this place, in copies transmitted to them, he finishes with the words 'I bless and exalt the blessed Creator for all His works.'

This is the end of the history of Nebuchadnezzar. Then he proceeds to tell us the history of Belshazzar, his grandson;

74

the history of his son Evil Merodach is omitted, because no act was done by him like those done by his father and his son Belshazzar. Of Evil Merodach, we only hear of the kindness that he showed to Jehoiakin. He was, probably, the best of them.

V

King Belshazzar gave a great banquet for his thousand nobles, and in the presence of the thousand he drank wine. [2]Under the influence of the wine, Belshazzar ordered the gold and silver vessels that his father Nebuchadnezzar had taken out of the temple at Jerusalem to be brought so that the king and his nobles, his consorts, and his concubines could drink from them.

V.

1. Belshazzar reigned three years at least. He made this feast at the end of the time (ver. 3, *inf.*). The book does not explain why the feast was made. He may have counted the seventy years which God had appointed for them; and when he saw the seventy years were completed, and the kingdom remained unchanged, he made the feast out of joy, thinking that all which had been said had fallen to the ground. This was why he dared to take the vessels of the house of God which Nebuchadnezzar his father had put away, and abstained from employing. When Belshazzar saw the seventy years completed and the kingdom remaining, he said, 'These vessels are mine and there is no return:' so he began to praise his gods, in whom he now believed. He was too hasty; though, and this was one of the causes of his ruin. He did not invite any besides the nobles, their attendants and followers; who, he tells us, were a **thousand** souls. **And in the presence of the thousand he drank wine**: they were in his hall, and he drank in their presence.

2. **While he tasted the wine**: some say that his intoxication excited him to this, whereas, had he been sober he would not have done so, but would have refrained from bringing them out and drinking out of them. Others suggest that, while the wine was pleasant to him, he wished to drink out of the vessels of the house of God, these being vessels fit to drink out of, such as 'cups' and 'bowls,' etc.

76

Golden and silver vessels in ver. 2; in ver. 3 the *silver* is omitted: either for brevity; there being no doubt, if the gold were brought, that the silver would be brought too; or he may have ordered them, and afterwards preferred the gold exclusively. Then they praised the god[s] of the images; and did not praise the blessed Creator, despising Him in their hearts, and thinking that they were masters of the vessels of the house of God. Just then came the term which God had fixed.

³The golden vessels that had been taken out of the sanctuary of the House of God in Jerusalem were then brought, and the king, his nobles, his consorts, and his concubines drank from them. ⁴They drank wine and praised the gods of gold and silver, bronze, iron, wood, and stone. ⁵Just then, the fingers of a human hand appeared and wrote on the plaster of the wall of the king's palace opposite the lamp stand, so that the king could see the hand as it wrote. ⁶The king's face darkened, and his thoughts alarmed him; the joints of his loins were loosened and his knees knocked together. ⁷The king called loudly for the exorcists, Chaldeans, and diviners to be brought. The king addressed the wise men of Babylon, "Whoever can read this writing and tell me its meaning shall be clothed in purple and wear a golden chain on his neck, and shall rule as ᵃ⁻one of three⁻ᵃ in the kingdom."

5. **The fingers of a man's hand**: this shows that he saw a hand appear, but did not see the arm, or the person. So, too, Ezekiel (8.3) saw a hand only; and likewise Daniel on a later occasion (10.7).

On the plaster of the wall of the palace: referring to the white plaster. The writing was black, so that it showed. The king saw it alone of those who were in the hall, just as Nebuchadnezzar only saw Hananiah, Mishael, Azariah, and the angel.

6. When he saw this miracle, he was filled with fear, and shaking came upon him. Owing to the greatness of his terror, the vertebrae of his spine were loosened, and his knees struck against each other.

7. He immediately summoned the wise men to tell him the writing and its interpretation; promising the person who would read it, and show him the interpretation, to clothe him in royal garments, and put a gold chain about his neck, while a herald cried before him that he was LORD over a third part

---

ᵃ⁻ *Cf. Dan. 6.3; or "third in rank."*
⁻ᵃ *Cf. Dan. 6.3; or "third in rank."*

of the kingdom. This is like what Pharaoh did to Joseph, only he entrusted his affairs to Joseph without making him a partner in the kingdom, whereas Belshazzar meant that of all the taxes that came to him Daniel should have a third part, and a third in every benefit which the king enjoyed. His grandfather Nebuchadnezzar had made no such offer to the person who would tell him his dream and its interpretation, but had merely offered presents, rewards, and dignities, inferior to the sovereignty. This was because this matter made more impression on Belshazzar than the other had made, and because of the fright, fear, and impatience that had seized him.

⁸Then all the king's wise men came, but they could not read the writing or make known its meaning to the king. ⁹King Belshazzar grew exceedingly alarmed and his face darkened, and his nobles were dismayed. ¹⁰Because of the state of the king and his nobles, the queen came to the banquet hall. The queen spoke up and said, "O king, live forever! Let your thoughts not alarm you or your face darken.

8. The writing was not unlike any existing writing. On the contrary, it was an existing character, whether Hebrew or some other. The answer (to the problem) is that the letters were not *arranged* in order, but inverted, the letters of xnm being arranged mnx: and similarly all the letters of the four words were transposed. Consequently, the wise men did not understand them: and, when they read them, they got no intelligible word, much less its interpretation. Belshezzar's heart was close to breaking at this. When Daniel, after the others had failed, read it and interpreted it, he was able to address him as he did in presence of the multitude, and explain to him his sin and the wickedness of his conduct, as described at the outset of the chapter.

9. He had hoped that his wise men would understand it, and tell him its interpretation: so when they did not understand it, his horror increased and his color changed. It is not improbable that he saw the hand while the others did not see it, and that on account of this they were astonished and confounded when he said, 'I see a great hand which has written this, and terror confounds me!'

10. This **queen** was his grandmother, wife of Nebuchadnezzar, and was acquainted with these matters from their beginning.

By reason of the words of the king: this refers to the terror and fright that had seized the king, the change of the expression on his face, the bewilderment of his nobles, and [the fears] that had fallen on them because of the king's

80

reaction - from this their joy had been changed into this plight. Her heart pained her on his account, since he was her son's son, now that this trouble had fallen upon him, and she feared that he might die of the fright which had beset his heart; at any rate that he would not rest until there came the person who had the power to read to him the writing and understand its interpretation.

¹¹There is a man in your kingdom who has the spirit of the holy gods in him; in your father's time, illumination, understanding, and wisdom like that of the gods were to be found in him, and your father, King Nebuchadnezzar, appointed him chief of the magicians, exorcists, Chaldeans, and diviners. ¹²Seeing that there is to be found in Daniel (whom the king called Belteshazzar) extraordinary spirit, knowledge, and understanding to interpret dreams, to explain riddles and solve problems, let Daniel now be called to tell the meaning [of the writing]."

11. She informs him that there is present in the city Daniel, who will read the writing, and interpret it to him; so he would cease from [the terror] that had fallen upon him. Then she began to recount to him some details of Daniel's wisdom, and how he was above all his father's wise men, having been the most eminent of them, so he would be convinced that Daniel would understand the writing, and a more difficult thing too. The most probable account of this matter is that Daniel had never come before him, and had never known him at all, having been absent from Babylon during this year (see on 8.1); after which he returned, very probably for this very purpose, providentially. Next she described Daniel to him so he would know him and his skill.

In verse 11 she ascribed to him four characteristics: (1) **spirit of the holy gods**; (2) **light**; (3) **understanding**; (4) **wisdom**. In the next verse she repeats some of them in the same words, and others with a change of expression. Probably an excellent spirit means the same as **spirit of the holy gods**; **knowledge** is the explanation of **wisdom like the wisdom of the gods**; **interpreting of dreams** the specification of light; this word Vryhn may either mean 'that which is correct' according to the Hebrew, or 'light' according to the Aramaic (cp. 11.22); meaning that he can uncover hidden things, which are as it were in dark places, so that they can be seen and understood.

An excellent spirit: referring to his inspiration, the like

82

of which was not to be found among the wise men of Babylon.

Knowledge: the philosophical sciences, as in 1.4.

Understanding: reasoning power.

Interpreting of dreams: referring to difficult dreams, as happened to him when he explained the tree (chap. 4).

Showing of dark sentences: this is not illustrated in the book. 'Dark sentences' are, in the language of the philosophers, unusual sayings constructed in a language made up of hints, like Samson's riddle.

¹³Daniel was then brought before the king. The king addressed Daniel, "You are Daniel, one of the exiles of Judah whom my father, the king, brought from Judah. ¹⁴I have heard about you that you have the spirit of the gods in you, and that illumination, knowledge, and extraordinary wisdom are to be found in you. ¹⁵Now the wise men and exorcists have been brought before me to read this writing and to make known its meaning to me. But they could not tell what it meant. ¹⁶I have heard about you, that you can give interpretations and solve problems. Now if you can read the writing and make known its meaning to me, you shall be clothed in purple and wear a golden chain on your neck and rule as one of three in the kingdom."

¹⁷Then Daniel said in reply to the king, "You may keep your gifts for yourself, and give your presents to others. But I will read the writing for the king, and make its meaning known to him.

12. **Dissolve knots**: a form of expression which is thought to be simple, but which the wise man can analyze into its parts. She added that his grandfather had set him above all his wise men because he possessed all these qualities; and that he also called him by the name of his god on that account.

13. The queen had not told him that Daniel was of the Jews. Possibly he asked those present about him, and they told him so. This remark of Belshazzar was not meant contemptuously at such a time: he must have said it to him because the Jews were famous for prophecy and the divine sciences.

16. He said in the first verse (14) 'that a spirit of the gods and light and prudence;' in the second (this verse) he adds 'solutions' also, according to what the queen had stated.

17. He would not accept any of the things he mentioned for several reasons. First, because he did not want his favors, which were not proportionate, but dictated by ignorance and insolence; secondly, because they were honors which would be annulled at once. Thirdly, that it might not be said that he had interpreted it for the sake of what he was going to get.

84

He said, 'I will not take from you, so, if you will give these gifts, give them to some one else, whom you may choose. I will read the writing and tell you its interpretation: that is your only desire and your request.'

¹⁸O king, the Most High God bestowed kingship, grandeur, glory, and majesty upon your father Nebuchadnezzar. ¹⁹And because of the grandeur that He bestowed upon him, all the peoples and nations of every language trembled in fear of him. He put to death whom he wished, and whom he wished he let live; he raised high whom he wished and whom he wished he brought low. ²⁰But when he grew haughty and willfully presumptuous, he was deposed from his royal throne and his glory was removed from him. ²¹He was driven away from men, and his mind made like that of a beast, and his habitation was with wild asses. He was fed grass like cattle, and his body was drenched with the dew of heaven until he came to know that the Most High God is sovereign over the realm of man, and sets over it whom He wishes. ²²But you, Belshazzar his son, did not humble yourself although you knew all this. ²³You exalted yourself against the Lord of Heaven, and had the vessels of His temple brought to you. You and your nobles, your consorts, and your concubines drank wine from them and praised the gods of silver and gold, bronze and iron, wood and stone, which do not see, hear, or understand; but the God who controls your lifebreath and every move you make—Him you did not glorify!

18-22. He prefaces this introduction to show him that he was not greater than his grandfather, who had reached in sovereignty, power, terror and majesty a height which his grandson had not reached. Still, when he grew proud, and became tyrannical, the Creator humbled him to a degree beyond which there was no further degradation. God raises the humble, humbles the proud, slays mighty kings, and does whatever else He will; and no one is able to oppose Him, or prevent His will.

22. **Though you knew all this**: showing that Belshazzar knew all that had happened to his grandfather, therefore he should have taken warning. He then tells him that his seizure of the vessels of God's house was impudence towards God and contempt of Him in his soul. Then Daniel looked towards the hall and the people there, and saw the vessels of the house of God, and how they had been used for drinking.

He told Belshazzar how they had been praising their gods, and had not praised God Almighty as was His due, but had praised instead the idols which can do nothing, being mere images and semblances. Then after showing him the inferiority of his gods, and his folly and audacity, he said to him, 'On account of these actions, the author of this writing was sent.'

²⁴He therefore made the hand appear, and caused the writing to be inscribed. ²⁵This is the writing that is inscribed: MENE MENE TEKEL UPHARSIN ²⁶And this is its meaning: MENE—God has numbered^b [the days of] your kingdom and brought it to an end; ²⁷TEKEL—^{c-}you have been weighed^{-c} in the balance and found wanting; ²⁸PERES—your kingdom ^{d-}has been divided^{-d} and given to the Medes and the Persians." ²⁹Then, at Belshazzar's command, they clothed Daniel in purple, placed a golden chain on his neck, and proclaimed that he should rule as one of three in the kingdom.
³⁰That very night, Belshazzar, the Chaldean king, was killed,

24-27. He tells him that on account of his actions, as described, the angel had been sent and had written these four words. He then combined the fifteen letters into words, mentioning numbers twice; the first referring to the number of years (seventy) which God had appointed for Nebuchadnezzar, his son, and his son's son (Jeremiah 27.7), the second to the reign of Belshazzar; The related sets of numbers are three (kings) and seventy (years). When these were completed, they had nothing more left. Tekel he interprets as you are weighed; implying that one who is *wanting* cannot be taken, but only one who is full weight; i.e. whose intelligence, wisdom, piety, etc. are so. Now, in his father and grandfather there had been a certain number of praiseworthy characteristics, but in him there were none; all his qualities were *wanting*. Pharsin he interprets as fragments, comparing him to a thing that is broken, wherein nothing reparable is left; referring to the destruction of all his supporters in the kingdom, and his own murder. This is why *Pharsin* is in the plural. It signifies his own destruction, i.e.

---

^b *Aramaic* ○ ⅏ ■ ♋.
^{c-} *Aramaic* ♦ ⅏ & ⅄ ● ♦ ♋.
^{-c} *Aramaic* ♦ ⅏ & ⅄ ● ♦ ♋.
^{d-} *Aramaic* □ ⅏ □ ⅄ • ♋ ♦.
^{-d} *Aramaic* □ ⅏ □ ⅄ • ♋ ♦.

death, and the destruction after him of all the supporters of the Chaldean rule. Then he informed him that that rule would be transferred to the *Medes and Persians.*

29. The king's promise to the one who interpreted the writing had to be fulfilled, necessarily; and Daniel could not resist, though he knew that this sovereignty was temporary.

30. Darius knew that a word spoken by Daniel would be fulfilled, and that the kingdom was destined for the Medes and Persians. It may be that Daniel had told him he and no other would be king, therefore he was encouraged to kill Belshezzar. Or he may have been killed by some of his servants. Scripture does not record who the murderer was.

and Darius the Mede received the kingdom, being about sixty-two years old. [2]It pleased Darius to appoint over the kingdom one hundred and twenty satraps to be in charge of the whole kingdom; [3]over them were three ministers, one of them Daniel, to whom these satraps reported, in order that the king not be troubled.

VI.

1-3. **Received the kingdom**: i.e. received it from the Chaldees; cp. *inf.* 9.50 We are not told how he was established in the sovereignty, nor how he became seated in Babylon on the royal throne. However, the writer tells us that Darius was born in the year in which Nebuchadnezzar took captive Jehoiakin king of Judah. This is to show that in the very year when he did so much to Jerusalem, and won so great a victory, God raised up someone against him, who would take his kingdom from him. For this reason we are given his age at the time when he received the kingdom from the Chaldees. Since there was no purpose in telling us the age of any of the other kings of the Gentiles or of the Israelites[?] at the time of their coming to the throne, it is nowhere else given.

Darius was certain that the kingdom was established in his hands, and that he did not have to march out to fight opponents. Therefore, he appointed these 120 governors - to each of whom belonged a particular province, where he left a viceroy - while he himself remained with the king in the capital. He appointed three presidents, who were over them. He appointed the 120 so they would govern the kingdom, and the king would not have to be fatigued with all the business. This is the same sort of plan as Pharaoh adopted when he appointed Joseph to govern the kingdom, giving himself up to amusement, and retaining merely the title.

3. With tywf cp. Jonah 1.6 and Psalms 146.4. He set the three presidents over the 120; and Daniel, who was one of the three, over both the governors and the presidents, so that none of them could do anything except with his consent. He did this, **because an excellent spirit was in him**. He was never found incompetent, nor his orders and counsels poor. So the king was, observe, *planning* to remove the others; and establish Daniel by himself; i.e. it was not practicable for him to establish Daniel at once; such a matter, he knew, required gentle strategy. So, he went to the chief nobles of the empire, and did not remove them from their high Station until his sovereignty was established. When it was established he began to plot to remove them little by little. When they perceived this, they began to plot to remove him from the kingdom altogether.

⁴This man Daniel surpassed the other ministers and satraps by virtue of his extraordinary spirit, and the king considered setting him over the whole kingdom. ⁵The ministers and satraps looked for some fault in Daniel's conduct in matters of state, but they could find neither fault nor corruption, inasmuch as he was trustworthy, and no negligence or corruption was to be found in him. ⁶Those men then said, "We are not going to find any fault with this Daniel, unless we find something against him in connection with the laws of his God." ⁷Then these ministers and satraps came thronging in to the king and said to him, "O King Darius, live forever! ⁸All the ministers of the kingdom, the prefects, satraps, companions, and governors are in agreement that a royal ban should be issued under sanction of an oath that whoever shall address a petition to any god or man, besides you, O king, during the next thirty days shall be thrown into a lions' den. ⁹So issue the ban, O king, and put it in writing so that it be unalterable as a law of the Medes and Persians that may not be abrogated."

4. The presidents and governors agreed together by reason of their envy of Daniel, which had penetrated their hearts. The king, they said, has only exalted him above us owing to the excellence of his counsel. We must plan some device to convince the king of some error or shortcoming of his, so he will remove him from power altogether. They sought, he says, for an error, but could not find one.

Error or mischief: 'error' means oppression of the subjects, 'Mischief,' wrong done in reference to the king, or wasting the revenue.

5. Despairing of finding a way to attack Daniel on the side of the king, they thought they would be able to trap him in the matter of the worship of his LORD. Their intention was not to show that he neglected any of his religious duties, but of another sort.

7-9. **Have consulted together**: indicating that they had assembled and consulted about a measure which would establish the king in his rule, so the people would obey him;

92

and that it was necessary this should be done. If the king failed to do it, his kingdom would become insecure. They bound themselves to this, in order that Daniel might not be able to serve God, which was their real object. This, the king did not know: which was part of their treachery against him. Had the king known, he would not have agreed to their counsel nor accepted it, nor set his signature. Then they said to him, 'Set your signature so it may be read to the people in the streets and in the assemblies, and none of them may oppose it.' They included in their phrase that **every man**, the followers of every religion, should be subject to this, not confining the law to religions other than their own. This was a stroke of policy, to make it apply to Daniel. They appointed it for the space of **thirty days**, to make it last long; that being with them the maximum amount of time they could refrain from worship of their deity. Had that not been allowed by their religion, he would not have enacted it. They also forbade people to make any request of each other, as they had forbidden them to make any of God; but their object was only the latter. They this did so that none other than themselves would know their purpose. Then they exempt *the king* for two reasons. First, because it was absolutely necessary; otherwise the nation would have perished from mutual outrages and difficulties. Secondly, they exalted the king above all gods to magnify his estate. All this was to show him that by this statute his kingdom would be confirmed and set in order. When the king saw that they were agreed about it, it was clear to him that, unless he did what they requested, his power would be shaken. So, he did it. He did not take Daniel's opinion beforehand, because they had told him that it was a part of the administration where Daniel had absolutely no concern.

¹⁰Thereupon King Darius put the ban in writing.

¹¹When Daniel learned that it had been put in writing, he went to his house, in whose upper chamber he had had windows made facing Jerusalem, and three times a day he knelt down, prayed, and made confession to his God, as he had always done. ¹²Then those men came thronging in and found Daniel petitioning his God in supplication. ¹³They then approached the king and reminded him of the royal ban: "Did you not put in writing a ban that whoever addresses a petition to any god or man besides you, O king, during the next thirty days, shall be thrown into a lions' den?" The king said in reply, "The order stands firm, as a law of the Medes and Persians that may not be abrogated."

11. Daniel may have known what was in their minds, and their purpose, i.e. that he and no other was their mark. He knew, as well, what the king had done. However, he did not tell the king, trusting to the Creator of all. He mentions the **windows**, because they looked in at him through them, surprised him, and behold he was praying.

Towards Jerusalem: this does not mean that the windows were opened towards Jerusalem, but rather that he stood facing Jerusalem, the Qiblah.

As he did before: showing that it was not a thing which he began then. It implies that he had regularly done so, and that it is an obligatory duty, which cannot be neglected. The **three times** probably mean evening, morning, and midday. From the words he **knelt on his knees** we learn that this is one condition of prayer (cp. Psalms 45.6).

12. Doubtless he had perceived that they had come to see him. He did not, however, interrupt his prayer, but continued until the end, so that when they came upon him he was still praying. These men were the governors and presidents.

13. His answer, **the thing is true**, means 'it is so,' and none may transgress it. Whoever transgresses will be cast

into a den of lions. When they heard this saying of the king, and had reminded him of his decree, they proceeded.

14. **Of the children of the captivity**: contemptuous, indicating that he was of the vilest of the people: 'yet you have raised him above them all, and he has opposed your command, and loosened that with which you have bound the nation.' After this speech, they wanted the king to order that Daniel be thrown into the den of lions.

¹⁴Thereupon they said to the king, "Daniel, one of the exiles of Judah, pays no heed to you, O king, or to the ban that you put in writing; three times a day he offers his petitions [to his God]." ¹⁵Upon hearing that, the king was very disturbed, and he set his heart upon saving Daniel, and until the sun set made every effort to rescue him. ¹⁶Then those men came thronging in to the king and said to the king, "Know, O king, that it is a law of the Medes and Persians that any ban that the king issues under sanction of oath is unalterable."

15. When he heard them say that the violator of the decree was Daniel, he saw that they had laid the plot against him: so he began to make excuses for Daniel; such as that he did not count as one of the multitude to whom the prohibition applied: 'since he is the ruler of the kingdom, and the people intended were others?' This and similar things he kept saying to them until sunset, opposing their proposition and excusing Daniel. Some have supposed that he said to them, 'Daniel cannot have known what was written. Had he heard of it, he would not have disobeyed our decree.' Nevertheless, when the sun set, Daniel rose and prayed, and the king no longer had any excuse for him.

16. In other words: 'If Daniel is not cast into the lions' den, the rule of the Medes and Persians will have been broken. Now, if it can be broken in Daniel's case, it can be broken in other cases. This is a principle which will extend itself to all men; and the kingdom will be ruined.' Their meaning was, that if the king altered their laws they would revolt against him, seeing that it was quite impossible that one who altered their laws should be king over them.

17. Darius' language is very different from that of Nebuchadnezzar (*sup*. 3.15). Darius believed in God's power to deliver Daniel in some miraculous manner, whereas Nebuchadnezzar believed in no such power. The sparks of fire killed those who threw the victims into the furnace (in the case of Shadrach, etc.,), because they were close to it.

Those who threw Daniel into the den of lions did not suffer in the same way; the lions were far away from them. Darius said to Daniel at the moment of his being thrown in, 'Doubtless the God whom you serve continually will save you from the lions, since He is able to do this. Those who have plotted against you will not see their designs fulfilled.'

[17]By the king's order, Daniel was then brought and thrown into the lions' den. The king spoke to Daniel and said, "Your God, whom you serve so regularly, will deliver you." [18]A rock was brought and placed over the mouth of the den; the king sealed it with his signet and with the signet of his nobles, so that nothing might be altered concerning Daniel.

[19]The king then went to his palace and spent the night fasting; no diversions were brought to him, and his sleep fled from him. [20]Then, at the first light of dawn, the king arose and rushed to the lions' den.

18. Probably the den had a door, through which the lions were let in; and also a mouth where their food was thrown to them, when there was no man thrown. It was these people's duty, when any man had condemned to death, to throw him to the lions. It was Nebuchadnezzar's way to kill by fire, and of the rest to kill by the sword.

That nothing might be changed concerning Daniel: he means lest, when they saw that the lions did not harm Daniel, they, themselves, might stone him, and kill him; since they now dealt openly with him. The king did this because he knew that God Almighty would deliver him; otherwise he would not have sealed the stone, which was at the top of the pit.

19. tVm is the Chaldee for the Hebrew Wx yLc. His heart burned for Daniel, so that he refused music and pleasure. Because his thoughts were occupied with him, he thought much concerning him, and his could not sleep, so that he got no rest until dawn.

20. sqq. He arose at dawn, his mind deep in thought. Then he called to Daniel so he would respond, and delight his heart with [an assurance of] his safety.

[21]As he approached the den, he cried to Daniel in a mournful voice; the king said to Daniel, "Daniel, servant of the living God, was the God whom you served so regularly able to deliver you from the lions?" [22]Daniel then talked with the king, "O king, live forever! [23]My God sent His angel, who shut the mouths of the lions so that they did not injure me, inasmuch as I was found innocent by Him, nor have I, O king, done you any injury." [24]The king was very glad, and ordered Daniel to be brought up out of the den. Daniel was brought up out of the den, and no injury was found on him, for he had trusted in his God.

My God has sent His angel: to be taken literally. God Almighty sent His angel to deliver him, as He sent His angel to Hananiah, Mishael and Azariah. Although the lions were hungry, He kept them from harming him.

because as before Him innocence: referring to his righteous conduct in matters between himself and God generally, and also to what was said above, ver. 4.

And also before you, O king, I have done no hurt: indicating that he had done nothing to earned this treatment.

24. They let down ropes, as was done in the case of Jeremiah.

²⁵Then, by order of the king, those men who had slandered Daniel were brought and, together with their children and wives, were thrown into the lions' den. They had hardly reached the bottom of the den when the lions overpowered them and crushed all their bones.

²⁶Then King Darius wrote to all peoples and nations of every language that inhabit the earth, "May your well-being abound! ²⁷I have hereby given an order that throughout my royal domain men must tremble in fear before the God of Daniel, for He is the living God who endures forever; His kingdom is indestructible, and His dominion is to the end of time; ²⁸He delivers and saves, and performs signs and wonders in heaven and on earth, for He delivered Daniel from the power of the lions."

25. These men were the 122 who had plotted against him. Every one who had displayed any hatred towards Daniel they included with them: also their sons and wives; because it was the rule in Persian law to include the women and children with the men; or perhaps their wives and their grown-up sons had displayed some joy at Daniel's misfortune and hatred towards him, and so had earned their fate in the king's mind. Probably they threw them down in parties according to the number of the lions, each lion getting one; and when they saw that he had devoured him, they produced another until they had devoured them all. Then Daniel returned to the administration of the kingdom by himself, as the king had originally intended (ver. 3). Doubtless the king's written statute must have held good until the end of the thirty days, except [for] Daniel and those who, like him, were worshippers of God Almighty.

26 sqq. Darius acted as Nebuchadnezzar had done, when he returned from the wilderness to his throne, in circulating letters, recounting what had happened to him. He felt bound to magnify the blessed Creator and publish His miracles; and to command mankind to fear Him; He being the eternal God,

Whose kingdom and prevailing sovereignty never cease; and the Savior and Deliverer of whom He chooses.

Works signs and wonders in heaven and earth: signs in the heavenly hosts, such as eclipses, etc.; and in earth, such as took place in the history of Daniel and his companions. Darius himself had witnessed this, and knew it. Then he informed them how Daniel had been cast into the lions' den, and had not been hurt. Doubtless, people already knew what the 120 men had done until they were thrown to the lions, removed from office and others appointed in their stead.

²⁹Thus Daniel prospered during the reign of Darius and during the reign of Cyrus the Persian.

29. He was in power and office. (Cp. 1. *ad fin.*)

This is the end of the history of Nebuchadnezzar, Belshazzar, and Darius. The history of Cyrus and the Persian kings who succeeded him is told in the book of Ezra.

VII

In the first year of King Belshazzar of Babylon, Daniel saw a dream and a vision of his mind in bed; afterward he wrote down the dream. Beginning the account,

VII.

1. He was already acquainted with the facts about the *four kingdoms* contained in Nebuchadnezzar's dream, as explained by him. After this, however, he received fuller accounts of the same vision; part of which is contained in the now following dream, parts in chapters, 8, 9, 10 - in all five chapters. Now the dream which Nebuchadnezzar saw, and this dream which Daniel saw, mention all four kingdoms. The *Vision,* on the contrary, does not mention the first, but only three. The fourth chapter (chap. 9) contains a summary history of the Second Temple, and also a notice of what Rome, the fourth kingdom, did to Jerusalem. The fifth chapter describes the fortunes of the kings of Greece, Rome, and Arabia, etc., as we will explain with God's help. These four chapters, composed by the blessed Daniel, may be thus divided: the first consists of what he saw in the *dream* the second of what he saw in the *vision;* the third and fourth of what he saw when *awake;* indicating the high stage he had reached in prophecy. God Almighty revealed this to Daniel of all mankind, owing to his anguish at our sufferings, the

102

interest he felt in what was going to happen to us, and his *desire* to know how long the time would be. For this reason he is called the *man of desires*.

Then he wrote the dream: because he wanted it to have a place in the collection of documents written by the blessed prophets.

And told the sum of the matter: meaning either that he wrote down the important points of the dream; or else referring to the heading words in the chapter, **Daniel spoke, and said**, as they are written. This means that the events took place just as they are recorded in this book. This was so it would not be thought that only part of the dream was written, the dream being symbolized; since the prophets do sometimes write part [of a history] and omit part; as in the Books of Kings.

[2]Daniel related the following:

"In my vision at night, I saw the four winds of heaven stirring up the great sea. [3]Four mighty beasts different from each other emerged from the sea. [4]The first was like a lion but had eagles' wings. As I looked on, its wings were plucked off, and it was lifted off the ground and set on its feet like a man and given the mind of a man. [5]Then I saw a second, different beast, which was like a bear but raised on one side, and with three fangs in its mouth among its teeth; it was told, 'Arise, eat much meat!' [6]After that, as I looked on, there was another one, like a leopard, and it had on its back four wings like those of a bird; the beast had four heads, and dominion was given to it. [7]After that, as I looked on in the night vision, there was a fourth beast—fearsome, dreadful, and very powerful, with great iron teeth—that devoured and crushed, and stamped the remains with its feet. It was different from all the other beasts which had gone before it; and it had ten horns. [8]While I was gazing upon these horns, a new little horn sprouted up among them; three of the older horns were uprooted to make room for it. There were eyes in this horn like those of a man, and a mouth that spoke arrogantly.

2, 3. He saw four winds stirring the great sea, i.e. the ocean. After it had been stirred, there rose from it these four animals. Apparently, he must have thought in the dream that he was standing on the seashore until the animals rose. Then he begins to describe them one by one.

4-8. We must explain why these kingdoms are compared to animals. Sometimes they are compared to *horses* (Zechariah 6.1), which are domestic animals; and similarly *infra*. the king of Persia is compared, to a *ram,* and the king of Greece to a goat. In my opinion he (Zechariah) compared the four kingdoms to horses, because they are used in war. Since each of these kingdoms was at war with some other, he compared them to horses. Nebuchadnezzar he compares at one time to an eagle, at another to a lion; to an eagle as being the strongest bird of prey, and to a lion as being the strongest beast of prey. Similarly, none of the four kingdoms was more

104

powerful or braver than he. For a similar reason he compared him (chap. 11) to gold, which is more valuable than silver. The eagle again suggests the idea of flight and elevation; both of which apply to Nebuchadnezzar (Jeremiah 4:13 and Isaiah v. 27). The lion, too, has extraordinary strength, and never turns his back (Proverbs 30.30). In this verse he is compared to the two together. The *eagle's wings* are his mighty armies.

I was gazing: i.e. at the animal I saw with this terrible form, until I saw **its wings were plucked off**, so that it could not fly; typifying that his journeys and invasions were interrupted.

It was lifted up from the earth typifies what befell him during the seven years (4.30).

Set on its feet like a man and given the mind of a man: a description of his condition when his reason returned to him, he confessed the Unity of God, renounced tyranny and transgression, returned to his kingdom, and was increased in dignity above what he had possessed before (4 *ad fin.*). He describes Nebuchadnezzar only, not noticing the fortunes of his children, because they had no estate worth noticing, i.e., they achieved no acts of heroism or conquests; but only retained what was left them by Nebuchadnezzar.

Next, he describes the second animal, *as like to a bear*: referring to its stupidity; because they were believers in dualism and idolaters.

And it was raised up on one side: some take this literally, as meaning that as soon as it rose, it was in part overthrown; referring to its dealings with Israel, i.e. those of Darius with Daniel, of Cyrus, Darius the Persian, and Artaxerxes with Israel, and of Ahasuerus after the history of Haman.

And three ribs were in its mouth: i.e. they governed three quarters of the globe (cp. 8.4).

And they said thus to it, Arise, devour much flesh: the words of Haman (Esther 3.9). He does not say that it *ate*, because this design was not accomplished upon Israel, but was turned against their enemies. He describes, as we observed before, the conduct of the kings of Persia, but none of the Chaldean kings, except Nebuchadnezzar. Then he speaks of the third animal, which he compares to a *leopard;* the leopard being smaller than the bear. Similarly, in the last chapter he compares the kings of Persia to a ram, but those of Greece to a goat, which is smaller than a ram. Besides, the leopard haunts the doors of cities (Jeremiah 5.6); the *leopard* is the kings of Greece collectively.

Four wings of a bird: these are his (Cerasphorus') four disciples: see on 11.4.

And dominion was given to it: the well-known story of Alexander.

7. (**After this.**) Now he speaks of the *fourth animal,* which he does not compare, like the rest, to a known animal; because it had not any single religion or doctrine, nor did Daniel recognize in it any animal form, which he could compare it to. He can only tell of the horror, terror, and fear which it inspired. This is a description of the kingdom of Rome; cp. on 11. 40.

And it had great iron teeth: i.e. TITUS THE SINNER, and the others like him, who invaded cities and shed blood; as a wild beast tears with its teeth and tusks. The metaphor is followed up in it devoured (i.e. massacred), and broke in pieces (i.e. oppressed).

It was diverse: referring to the variety of its customs, and the great harm it did. **And it had ten horns**: i.e. ten thrones; see below on ver. 24.

8. **I considered the horns**: owing to their size. He was gazing intently on their size.

He looked, and, after this, this little horn had risen up amid the ten horns. When the little horn had come between them, three horns were thrown down before it. Seven were left, with this little horn among them. Then he perceived that this little horn had **eyes like the eyes of a man: and a mouth which spoke proud words**. He does not tell us what the words were; see below on ver. 25.

⁹As I looked on,
>Thrones were set in place,
>And the Ancient of Days took His seat.
>His garment was like white snow,
>And the hair of His head was like lamb's^a wool.
>His throne was tongues of flame;
>Its wheels were blazing fire.
>¹⁰A river of fire streamed forth before Him;
>Thousands upon thousands served Him;
>Myriads upon myriads attended Him;
>The court sat and the books were opened.

9. These thrones [which were cast down] are the kings mentioned above. The **Ancient of days** is an angel whose task it will be to judge the nations on the day of Judgement (cp. Psalms 1.3). **A throne of fire**, he tells us, was set up for him, and the wheels of his throne were **flaming fire**; the bodies of the supernal angels are of fire, and their thrones are of fire likewise. Then he showed him a **river of fire issuing out from before the angel**, with which he punished transgressors.

Thousands of thousands ministered to him: because he was the greatest of the angels, like the great Sultan, before whom stand a multitude of ministers. Then he tells us why he sat upon the throne with these ministers standing before him: **the judgment was set and the books were opened**: i.e. the judgement of the world for their denial of God (Deuteronomy 32.37). **The books were opened**: for some of their sins were of long standing, and their works were noted (ibid. 32). The expression refers to the ordinary custom of noting down a fact that may be of use after some time, so one may not forget it. He is using the language of the world. Compare for the same, in reference to the deeds of the wicked, Isaiah 45.6; and in reference to the conduct of the

---

^a *Or "clean."*

godly, Malachi 3.16 and Psalms 49.29. Reference is elsewhere made to God's judgment of the Gentiles for the wrong they have done Israel (Joel 3.2). He thought it appropriate to mention the Day of Judgment after the termination of the four kingdoms, to show that at the close of their rule they must expect judgment, punishment, and condemnation, and that their works are counted against them.

¹¹I looked on. Then, because of the arrogant words that the horn spoke, the beast was killed as I looked on; its body was destroyed and it was consigned to the flames. ¹²The dominion of the other beasts was taken away, but an extension of life was given to them for a time and season. ¹³As I looked on, in the night vision,

> One like a human being
> Came with the clouds of heaven;
> He reached the Ancient of Days
> And was presented to Him.

11. He returns to the history of the fourth animal. The cause of the destruction of this great creature, he tells us, was the proud language used by the horn; and though God Almighty gave it a long reprieve, yet every respite must end, and the time will at last have come.

(1) **The beast was slain,** (11) **his body destroyed,** and (3) **he was given to be burned with fire. Was slain** refers to the slaughter of their kings and the destruction of their armies. **And his body destroyed** most probably refers to the abolition of their worship and religions; so that there will not be left to them a Church or place of Direction (*Qiblah*). Or, it may mean the extinction of *Esau* from this world. **And he was given** refers to punishment in the next world, i.e. Gehenna, which means 'the place of condemnation.'

12. After narrating the destruction of the last animal, he records the cessation of the three kingdoms previously mentioned. This corresponds to 11.34, 5, *ubi vide.*

Yet their lives were prolonged: i.e. their religion and their remnants exist in spite of the dominance of other people and other systems.

For a season and a time: i.e. until the conclusion of the fourth kingdom; by a time is meant the dominion of Israel. So the remnants of the dominions and their cults will only pass away at the appearance of the blessed Messiah.

13. The Messiah is likened to a man, in contrast to the

110

four kingdoms, which were likened to beasts. This is for two reasons; one is, because he is *wise* and knows his LORD, a second, because he is LORD of all.

With the clouds of heaven: because God Almighty [will] send him, and men will witness him as they witness the clouds. Then we are told how he came to the angel who sat judging the people, and how the angel let him come before him, close to him. Then we are told how God gave the kingdom to him.

¹⁴Dominion, glory, and kingship were given to him;
All peoples and nations of every language must serve
    him.
His dominion is an everlasting dominion that shall not
    pass away,
And his kingship, one that shall not be destroyed.
¹⁵As for me, Daniel, my spirit was disturbed within me and the
vision of my mind alarmed me. ¹⁶I approached one of the
attendants and asked him the true meaning of all this. He gave
me this interpretation of the matter: ¹⁷' These great beasts, four
in number [mean] four kingdoms^b will arise out of the earth;

14. Three words are used of him: **dominion, glory,** and
kingdom. The first means the subjection of enemies and
rebels; the second, their coming to bow down to him at every
feast of Tabernacles, with splendid presents; the third, his
sitting on the royal throne, and receiving the tribute, and
writing mandates and signing with his name and seal. Then
he adds that his reign will never end - as that of the other
kingdoms ended, nor his rule die as theirs perished.

15. This describes his condition when he woke, and felt as
Nebuchadnezzar and others had felt when they did not know
how to interpret their dreams. A marvel that Daniel the
'interpreter of dreams' would not understand this! So, he slept
again, and saw angels, and asked them about its
interpretation. Or it may be supposed that it seemed to him
in the dream as if his *spirit was troubled,* and as if he was
confused by what he saw, and went to the angel who stood in
front of the great angel that sat upon the throne, to ask him
for the interpretation of the dream.

In the midst of the sheath: i.e. of the heart, which is like
the *sheath* to a sword (cp. 1 Chronicles 21.27).

16. **He told me** probably refers to what he said on the
subject of the four kingdoms; **the interpretation of the**

---

^b *Lit. "kings."*

112

speeches to the end of ver. 8 (cp. ver. 25). Or the first may refer to ver. 17, and the second to ver. 19.

¹⁸then holy ones of the Most High will receive the kingdom, and will possess the kingdom forever—forever and ever.' ¹⁹Then I wanted to ascertain the true meaning of the fourth beast, which was different from them all, very fearsome, with teeth of iron, claws of bronze, that devoured and crushed, and stamped the remains; ²⁰and of the ten horns on its head; and of the new one that sprouted, to make room for which three fell—the horn that had eyes, and a mouth that spoke arrogantly, and which was more conspicuous than its fellows. ²¹(I looked on as that horn made war with the holy ones and overcame them, ²²until the Ancient of Days came and judgment was rendered in favor of the holy ones of the Most High, for the time had come, and the holy ones took possession of the kingdom.)

17, 18. This is a general statement, without special explanation of the four animals. This corresponds to the method of both Joseph and Daniel in the interpretation of dreams; which is to give a general idea, resolving the knotty and difficult point. The *four animals* are interpreted as *four kingdoms,* and the *sea* as the *earth:* the **four winds** are not explained. They must be motions from God, whereat the four empires arose.

Will receive the kingdom explains ver. 13. Daniel had no need to ask about the first three animals, but only about the fourth.

19-22. He asked him concerning four things: (1) the signification of the fourth animal, its strength, its teeth, nails and devouring; (11) the nature of the ten horns; (3) the nature of the little horn and its eyes, and how it outgrew the ten horns; (4) the conduct of this horn in its wars, that he saw, with the saints, and its prevailing against them. He did not have a satisfactory understanding of any of these things. In Daniel's question to the angel there are certain things additional to what was mentioned in the vision - four: (1) **nails of brass;** (2) **a compounded horn;** (3) **whose look was more stout than his fellows;** (4) **made war with the**

114

saints. Furthermore, there are four verses about which he did not ask (9, 10, 11, 12), because he already understood their meaning. When he had asked about these riddles, the angel answered.

²³This is what he said: 'The fourth beast [means]—there will be a fourth kingdom upon the earth which will be different from all the kingdoms; it will devour the whole earth, tread it down, and crush it. ²⁴And the ten horns [mean]—from that kingdom, ten kings will arise, and after them another will arise. He will be different from the former ones, and will bring low three kings.

23, 24. Observe that he says of the fourth **diversified**. All four were already said to be *diverse the one from the other*, in their forms, as individually described. This fourth is made different from the others in respect of certain characteristics recorded in ver. 7.

Will devour the whole earth: i.e. after devastating Jerusalem and taking the people captive, they increased their dominion above all mankind. The ten horns are **ten kings**: i.e. ten thrones, belonging to Rome, on each of which a governor sat.

And another will arise after them: i.e. some years after the appearance of the ten horns. It rose up, he tells us, between the ten horns; i.e. in the midst of their dominion; and took out of their territory *three* thrones; according to some, ALEXANDRIA, JERUSALEM, and Acco.

And he will be different from the former: in his own opinion; for he ascended into heaven and seated himself on His right hand, and did other things that we cannot repeat, but which are well known to all, and which we need net explain. Of him it was said, 'they have set their mouth in heaven' (Psalms 73.9). This is the explanation of **a mouth speaking great things**. Then he explains the meaning of **and made war with the saints and prevailed against them**, sc. **he will wear out the saints of the Most High**: referring to the lowering of their rank, their humiliation and degradation in all departments in matters spiritual and temporal, beyond what preceded. This refers also to their having to wear the yellow badge, and being unable to speak

116

when reviled, or to walk on a Moslem's right, or to present themselves to buy goods however dear the price they offer for them, etc., etc. Then the angel added a fact about which he had not asked: and he **will hope to change**. Notice that he says 'and he will hope.' He does not say that he will change these for them, only that he will hope to do so. This hope will not be realized, because God Almighty will give him power to humble and oppress them in worldly matters, but will not give him power to annul their religion.

²⁵He will speak words against the Most High, and will harass the holy ones of the Most High. He will think of changing times and laws, and they will be delivered into his power for a ^ctime, times, and half a time.^{-c}

25. **Times and the law**: i.e. the holy-days, Sabbaths, and feasts. He says to change, not 'to abolish,' because he will not altogether abolish them, but only hope to *change* them, obliging them to do work which is unlawful for them on the Sabbaths and feast-days. **The law** may be the Qiblah, and certain forms of religious observances (compare Esther 3.8, where the king's 'laws' refer to the order to kneel down and make obeisance before Haman): or the *days of Purim* and similar Israelite institutions. It is not fully explained. The prophecy **and he will wear out the saints of the Most High** is now *in course of fulfillment* upon Israel. Of the other, **and he will hope**, probably part was fulfilled at his (Mohammed's) first appearance. The greater part, however, will be fulfilled in the 'time of tribulation,' as, by God's help, we will explain in the last chapter.

And they will be given into his hand until a time, times and half a time: until may either mean *until he have completed a time, times and half time*, that being the length of his reign, from beginning to end. It may mean that the tribulation mentioned in ver. 15 b will proceed from him over Israel for that period. Observe that he says **a time**, i.e. one time; and *times* in the plural, which need not refer exclusively to two, but to three or any larger number. Similarly in *half a time* the word is like the Hebrew ycH, which does not signify 'a half' exactly, but *a portion* of the thing called Ndf, etc.; as in Isaiah 44.16, where *half thereof* (he burns in the fire) [is shown] by what follows [to mean not exactly a half]. So *inf.* 12.7: *'a*

---

^{c-} *I.e., a year, two years, and a half a year.*
^{-c} *I.e., a year, two years, and a half a year.*

118

season, seasons and a half,' which is the same period as this, not another. We will explain that passage, God willing, recording the opinions of the learned, and stating what we ourselves believe most probable.

²⁶Then the court will sit and his dominion will be taken away, to be destroyed and abolished for all time. ²⁷The kingship and dominion and grandeur belonging to all the kingdoms under Heaven will be given to the people of the holy ones of the Most High. Their kingdom shall be an everlasting kingdom, and all dominions shall serve and obey them.' " ²⁸Here the account ends.

26. **The judgment will sit** refers probably to ver. 10 c, and tells us that at the end of a time, times, etc., no control will remain with any except God's angel, who will judge the nations for their doings; 5. *supra*.

And they will take away his dominion: i.e. of the kingdom whose treatment of Israel has been mentioned in ver. 25.

They will take away: i.e. either *Israel* will take away, according to the original idea given in 11.34; or the *Carmathians*, i.e. the 'Arms' (11.31), will take away, as we will explain in the last chapter.

To the end: showing that it will not, like Israel, have a return.

27. **Of the kingdoms**: even if there are other kingdoms in the world besides Rome and Arabia. All of them will obey the *kingdom of God,* i.e. of His people, and of His Messiah. **Their kingdom, too, will not pass away**: cp. Isaiah 9.6; Psalms 72.17. The prophets expand on this in numerous places.

The saints of the Most High (plural) in this chapter: either the *saints* are Israel, and *the Most High* the Creator (cp. HxLf xhLx, 3.26, etc.); and Israel being Holy to the LORD, they can be called [by a double plural] saints of the Most High. The *Most High* may be Israel, since God has made them supreme; cp. Deuteronomy 26.19.

28. **Here the account ends**: i.e. this was the last word spoken to me. After this I began to ponder on what I had

seen.

And I kept the word in my heart: i.e. the interpretation, so he would ask more about it, he wrote down the dream at once (*sup.* ver. 1), but not the interpretation. This is what happened to him in the first year of Belshazzar. Now he tells us what happened in the **third year**.

VIII

In the third year of the reign of king Belshazzar a vision appeared to me, even to me, Daniel, after that which appeared to me at the first. [2]I saw in the vision; now it was so, that when I saw, I was in Shushan the palace, which is in the province of Elam; and I saw in the vision, and I was by the river Ulai.

VIII.

1. The reason why he wrote the Dream in Aramaic, but the Vision in Hebrew has been supposed to be that he saw the dream when in Babylon, and the vision in Shushan the Capital. He was not with the king; see chap. 5, which shows that Daniel was absent from Babylon and at Shushan Habbirah. He does not tell us the reason of his absence. It has been suggested that when he saw the dream he left the city until the seventy years of Babylon would have been accomplished, and returned on Darius' account. He must have seen the vision at the beginning or in the middle of the year.

After that which appeared to me at the first: i.e. after the dream. As this, however, is shown already by § a, the words indicate that after this there were no more 'dreams' or 'visions' concerning the kingdoms.

1. He saw things like those he might see when asleep; but he was awake, and in the actual presence of certain objects that he could see, although they were not really to be seen. He says: 'I saw this vision when I was in Shushan Habbirah, and I saw myself in the vision standing on the river Ulai;' just as Ezekiel, when in Babylon, saw himself in Jerusalem.

LbVx= *river* cp. LbVy, Jeremiah 17.5. In the last chapter he is on the river Tigris.

³I looked and saw a ram standing between me and the river; he had two horns; the horns were high, with one higher than the other, and the higher sprouting last. ⁴I saw the ram butting westward, northward, and southward. No beast could withstand him, and there was none to deliver from his power. He did as he pleased and grew great. ⁵As I looked on, a he-goat came from the west, passing over the entire earth without touching the ground. The goat had a conspicuous horn on its forehead. ⁶He came up to the two-horned ram that I had seen standing between me and the river and charged at him with furious force. ⁷I saw him reach the ram and rage at him; he struck the ram and broke its two horns, and the ram was powerless to withstand him. He threw him to the ground and trampled him, and there was none to deliver the ram from his power. ⁸Then the he-goat grew very great, but at the peak of his power his big horn was broken. In its place, four conspicuous horns sprouted toward the four winds of heaven. ⁹From one of them emerged a small horn, which extended itself greatly toward the south, toward the east, and toward the beautiful land. ¹⁰It grew as high as the host of heaven and it hurled some stars of the [heavenly] host to the ground and trampled them. ¹¹It vaunted itself against the very chief of the host; on its account the regular offering was suspended, and His holy place was abandoned. ¹²ᵃ⁻An army was arrayed iniquitously against the regular offering;⁻ᵃ it hurled truth to the ground and prospered in what it did.

¹³Then I heard a holy being speaking, and another holy being said to whoever it was who was speaking, "How long will [what was seen in] the vision last—ᵃthe regular offering be forsaken because of transgression; the sanctuary be surrendered and the [heavenly] host be trampled?"⁻ᵃ ¹⁴He answered me,ᵇ "For twenty-three hundred evenings and mornings; then the sanctuary shall be cleansed."

3-14. We must first give the chapter its literal

ᵃ⁻ *Meaning of Heb. uncertain*
⁻ᵃ *Meaning of Heb. uncertain*
ᵃ⁻ *Meaning of Heb. uncertain*
⁻ᵃ *Meaning of Heb. uncertain*
ᵇ *Several ancient versions "him."*

interpretation, to be followed by the interpretation of the angel, and then combine the two together, as we did with the Dream. He saw then, in the Vision, a mighty ram standing on the bank of the river, on which there rose first one horn, then another afterwards. The second horn was greater than the first. Then he beheld wild beasts that fell on it from three-quarters,-the river being to its east,-and, it butted every animal that confronted it; and met none, but it did with each animal what it chose. Probably he saw the animals at first powerful and ferocious, and afterwards found that they had all died; and that none stood up before the ram. He remained alone, when this he-goat approached him from the western quarter with speed, not approaching on the ground, but moving in mid-air. Others suppose that none of the beasts approached the ground for fear of this he-goat. And he saw that it had a horn of a mighty *bearing* between its eyes; and that it made for the ram. When it saw that the ram neither feared it nor moved from its place, then the he-goat came upon it fast, when it was standing by itself on the bank of the river, and came close to it, to see whether it would run away, or butt with its horns. And, the ram was left quite alone. Then we are told that the he-goat was **moved with anger against it**, which means that he grew angry when he saw how the wild beasts and other animals had fled from before him and hidden themselves, but the ram remained in its place and did not flee. So, he made for the ram and killed it. Apparently the he-goat didn't harm any of the other beasts, because they did not stand before him. When he saw the ram stand, he fought with him, and butted his horns with his great horn. There was not enough force in the ram to meet him, so he threw him on the ground and trampled on him. Then he saw that the passers-by noticed what the he-goat had done, but did not rescue the ram; it did not have enough strength to rescue itself, nor could it find any one to rescue it: so the he-goat *killed* it. Then he tells us what happened to the he-goat: he **magnified himself exceedingly** and rose up. After he had magnified himself, he found that the great horn was broken without any beast or man breaking it: just as he had broken the horn of the ram. Then he saw how, after it was broken, there rose up four horns in its stead. These four were not attached the one to the other, but were in separate quarters. One was on the left, another on the right, another between the eyebrows over the top of the nose, and another at the top of the forehead, **to the four winds of heaven**. Then he saw how one horn issued from the midst of one of the four, i.e. the one that proceeded from his right temple: **Out of one of them came a forth a horn**.

From a little one: i.e. the one of the four horns from which it issued was the least of the four, and he saw this horn that had issued was magnified and increased above the height of the four horns. He saw it slanting in the direction now of the south, now of the west, now of the land of Israel. Then it seemed to him as though it had risen to the host of heaven, and thrown some of them down. **The host of heaven** very likely refers to the signs of the Zodiac; and **some of the stars** to some of the seven planets, *Sat-rn,* etc. Then it seemed to him as though it trampled the stars on the ground; and then as though the horn went to the Captain of the host and the mightiest of it. He does not say, though, that the horn did anything with the Captain of the host other than that it magnified itself.

And it took away from him the continual: as though the Captain of the host had a place in the earth which he frequented; and he was now excluded from there, and the pillar that stood there was cast on the ground and destroyed. It seemed to him as though part of the host that had not been trampled down by the horn was seized, together with the place which he used to visit, by the horn. He calls the horn sin, because he saw in the vision how the horn had with-drawn from the place and exalted itself. It seemed to him as though it came to certain people who spoke the truth, and threw them on the ground and thrust them through: and that it stood firm, and none came to break it. When he had seen these things, he saw two angels standing opposite him, and heard one ask the other 'How long?' This he did not ask to find out for himself. He did it so that Daniel would hear him. We learn this from his saying afterwards, **he said to me**, not 'to him;' as though the angel knew that he desired to understand this, just as he had desired to understand the meaning of the dream. He had been able to speak to those angels (7.16), but he did not have the courage to ask them. So the one asked the other about that which Daniel needed to ask. Now he did not ask about the whole Vision, but selected such future events as Israel needed to know; i.e. *the end of the four kingdoms.*

Then I heard a holy one speaking: i.e. the one who asks **How long? To Palmoni who spoke: Palmoni** is the answerer: the name of the asker is not given, like the names of many of the angels.

The asker says: **How long?** i.e. how long will this person last who will do the things mentioned in the verse, which are *three?* (1) **giving**; (2) **the sanctuary**; (3) **the host**. The answer in ver. 14 will be explained below.

¹⁵While I, Daniel, was seeing the vision, and trying to understand it, there appeared before me one who looked like a man. ¹⁶I heard a human voice from the middle of Ulai calling out, "Gabriel, make that man understand the vision." ¹⁷He came near to where I was standing, and as he came I was terrified, and fell prostrate. He said to me, "Understand, O man, that the vision refers to the time of the end." ¹⁸When he spoke with me, I was overcome by a deep sleep as I lay prostrate on the ground. Then he touched me and made me stand up, ¹⁹and said, "I am going to inform you of what will happen when wrath is at an end, for [it refers] to the time appointed for the end.
²⁰"The two-horned ram that you saw [signifies] the kings of Media and Persia;

15-18. He saw three angels, and heard their talk; and he heard the voice of one whom he did not see. He mentions the names of two, sc. **Palmoni** and **Gabriel**, but omits to mention the names of the other two. This shows that Daniel did not hear more than the question from the first two, owing to their great dreadfulness. Gabriel, however, looked like a man, so that Daniel felt more comfortable with him. He tells us that Gabriel did not begin speaking on his own, but only when he heard another commanding him to tell Daniel; after which he came to Daniel and told him. This indicates that the angels all knew. It is possible, however, that the angel whose voice he heard was more terrible than the two preceding (the *asker* and the *answerer*). When Gabriel approached him, Daniel **swooned** from fear of them, and then **fell fainting on his face**.

Understand, son of man: for the Vision belongs to the time of the end: i.e. you need to know this, because it contains information on what will be at the end of the Captivity.

18. **And he set me upright**: i.e. encouraged me and raised me up.

19. He now proceeds to summarize the contents of the

dream.

20. This is said generally, and we must interpret it further, as we have done in ether cases. He said in the Vision that the one horn was less than the other, i.e. the horn that came up first. This symbolizes the fact that Media was less in military power [and everything else]; their sole king being Darius the Mede, who reigned one year. From Persia, though, five kings arose, who reigned fifty-five years. The words **I saw the ram butting** (ver. 4) mean that he had armies which marched to the three quarters. This took place in the time of Cyrus, as is explained in Isaiah 45.1. With 4b compare *ibid.* 2.

²¹and the buck, the he-goat—the king of Greece; and the large horn on his forehead, that is the first king. ²²One was broken and four came in its stead—that [means]: four kingdoms will arise out of a nation, but without its power. ²³When their kingdoms are at an end, when the measure of transgression^c has been filled, then a king will arise, impudent and versed in intrigue.

21. We must again return to the contents of the dream that Gabriel did not explain. There came from the west: supposed to be *Alexander*, who came from, *Alexandria*. **And none touched the ground**: i.e. none confronted him from the time that he left Alexandria until he came to Babylon. He explains that the **great horn between his eyes** is Alexander, the first king. He goes on to describe what the he-goat did; **he smote the ram and broke his two horns**: i.e. he fought the two armies, sc. the force of Persia and Media; and he **cast him down to the ground**: referring to his conquering their territory, city by city, and slaying those of them who withstood him. Probably, he killed Artaxerxes the Persian, and when the news got into the provinces, none of them opposed Alexander any more.

And there was none that could deliver: i.e. none fought for them any more.

22, 23. He said above (ver. 8), and when he was strong, the great horn was broken: i.e. when Alexander had accomplished his purpose he became tyrannical, and thereafter was broken: i.e. died. Four notables he interprets as four kingdoms: i.e. four disciples who came after him, each of whom took possession of a quarter of the globe without any war breaking out among them at the beginning of their history.

Will stand up out of the nation: showing that these four are all Greeks. **Not with his power**: neither individually nor collectively will they have the strength of the first king. *Supra*,

---

^c *Lit. "transgressors."*

ver. 9, he said, **and out of one of them**: this is interpreted here, **In the latter time of their kingdom**: the full interpretation is not given until the great last chapter. Only **the one of them** is the **king of the south**, because the king of Arabia sprang up between them, as was shown in the Dream (7.8). To this matter we will come back, when we explain what the four kingdoms are. *ibid.*, ver. 9, from a little: indicating that the king of the south, at the time, was the least of the four disciples mentioned above. **And it slanted greatly towards the south**, etc.: i.e. none of the four got so far in any direction of the world as this horn did. **Towards the south**: i.e. according to some, *Amsar* to others, *Italy,'* to others, *Hijāz.* Towards the east: i.e. eastern countries and Khorasān generally. **And towards the pleasant land.**

Here he adds, **a king of fierce countenance, and understanding dark sentences**: referring to his boasting against God, and lying concerning Him. **Understanding dark sentences**: referring to his stealing from the books of the Jews, contradicting their assertions, and professing to be a prophet and to have received communications from Gabriel.

²⁴He will have great strength, but not through his own strength. He will be extraordinarily destructive; he will prosper in what he does, and destroy the mighty and the people of holy ones. ²⁵By his cunning, he will use deceit successfully. He will make great plans, will destroy many, taking them unawares, and will rise up against the chief of chiefs, but will be broken, not by [human] hands.

24b interprets 10 b. **Mighty ones**: i.e. *imperial personages,* Romans, and others with whom he fought and whose towns he took. **The people of the saints**: Israel. He does not say *all* the mighty ones and *all* the saints, because he was not monarch of the entire world.

And it cast down truth to the ground, of ver. 12, is explained **and he will corrupt wonderfully**: meaning that he railed against the Law of God and the words of his Prophets. He took what he pleased out of them, made up a book called the Koran, and declared the rest invalid.

Ver. 11 b is not explained here being perspicuous. The fact will be mentioned in the great last chapter.

Ver. 11 a. The **prince of the host** is interpreted here the **prince of princes**. This *prince of princes* may be the *king of Rome:* as he took three thrones of theirs, as was mentioned in chap. 7. Others think it refers to their viceroys in Babylon, in which case this will be the doing of the CONSPIRATOR who will rise against them *(inf.* 11.31). We will leave the explanation of this for the 4th chapter, and elucidate it there.

It did its pleasure and prospered, of ver. 12, is explained in ver. 24. The subject recurs in the long chapter, 5. and 11.3, where we will explain the terms **the continual** and the **place of his sanctuary**, sin, etc.

We are told here as well that **he will be broken without a hand**: This indicates that his power will diminish little by little, until he will die and pass away.

25. Having explained the chapter briefly, we will now return and mention certain things that will not recur. In the

131

first two chapters (i.e. 11 and 7) he speaks of *four* kingdoms, and the *reign of the Messiah*. In this chapter, he mentions nothing of the Chaldees. He only the three monarchies, which are the three beasts. To the description of the kingdom of Persia three details are added: (a) it is a divided kingdom, between Persia and Media: (b) **no beasts can stand before it**: *v. ad loc.*; (c) it will be slain by the he-goat, etc. These three things are to be connected with three things mentioned in chap. 7: (a) **it was raised up on one side**; (b) **three ribs were in its mouth**; (c) **thus they said to it, Arise, and eat much flesh**. There he describes how the three quarters got into its hands, and how people said to it, *Arise*, etc. By combining the two chapters we obtain a full account of the history of the Persian kingdom. Now let us mark what is said of the king of Greece. There he mentioned his *expeditions* (ver. 6: **it had on the back of it four wings of a fowl**) and its having four heads, corresponding to ver. 8 b. Here, he mentions **there came up four notable horns**: only we get additional illumination from the words (ver. 5) *and the goat had a notable horn*. This is because there he did not divide the kingdom, in order to make part of [the reign of] *the first kind*, and part [of] *the four disciples*.

The words **when the transgressors are come to the full** show that they will *transgress*, whether in matters of religion or in political matters: probably in the former.

He further adds to our knowledge of the **little horn** by calling him **king** (ver. 23). Ver. 24 is an addition to 7.25. As no further explanation was required of what had been said about the *day of Judgment* and the *reign of the Messiah* he leaves them out.

^{26}What was said in the vision about evenings and mornings is true. Now you keep the vision a secret, for it pertains to far-off days." ^{27}So I, Daniel, was stricken,[a] and languished many days. Then I arose and attended to the king's business, but I was dismayed by the vision and no one could explain it.

26. **The evenings and the mornings**: i.e. what you heard Palmoni say is to be taken literally. It is not an allegory like the Ram and the Goat (which are allegorical, and have to be interpreted, not meaning a Ram etc., in reality). No, these evenings and mornings are real evenings and mornings. You are not to suppose that the *evening* signifies a declining kingdom, and the *morning* a rising kingdom.

Two thousand three hundred: the sum made up by evenings and mornings combined: making IISO whole days. Notice that he does not say '2300 evenings and 2300 mornings' as elsewhere 'forty days and forty nights.'

But seal up the vision: i.e. there is no doubt about it. Some think it means *seal* this chapter, with its present contents.

For it belongs to many days: i.e. this is a thing that will come to pass after many long years.

27. Having heard in this vision that 'Truth would be cast to the ground,' etc., he was upset and distressed. **Days**: i.e. a year; until the death of Belshazzar.

Then I rose up and did the king's business: i.e. the office given him in the time of Darius. It was not his own choice. The king forced it on him.

And I was deserted: i.e. he kept aloof from society, cp. Ezekiel 3.15.

But there was none to make it understood: i.e. God Almighty did not reveal to him any of the things in his mind until the first year of Darius. Two years must have passed

---

[a] *Meaning of Heb. uncertain*

between the *Dream* and the *Vision*, the former being in the first year of Belshazzar, the latter in the third year. Then passed the third year of Belshazzar. So the narrative recorded in the next chapter must have been at the end of the year.

IX

In the first year of Darius son of Ahasuerus, of Median descent, who was made king over the kingdom of the Chaldeans—²in the first year of his reign, I, Daniel, consulted the books concerning the number of years that, according to the word of the LORD that had come to Jeremiah the prophet, were to be the term of Jerusalem's desolation—seventy years. ³I turned my face to the Lord God, devoting myself to prayer and supplication, in fasting, in sackcloth and ashes.

IX.

1. Probably after he had been cast into the den of lions. Darius' father's name is mentioned, because he was a noteworthy person. He was not, though, the Ahasuerus of Mordecai and Esther; the latter was a Persian and the present one of the Medes.

Who was made king: to show that the same person is meant as in chap. 5. *ult.*

2. Owing to the length of the sentence, the first year is repeated.

Of his reign: interpretation of in the first year of Darius.

I understood by the books: i.e. the books of Jeremiah. Jeremiah mentions it in a number of places (e.g. 25.1, 4, 29.10).

For the accomplishing of the desolations of Jerusalem: it had only been waste from the nineteenth year of king Nebuchadnezzar. At this period it had been waste fifty-two years. He can therefore only have meant seventy years *of the rule of Babylon*. The words *for the accomplishing* must therefore mean *after the seventy years of Babylon had been completed.*

3. When Daniel noticed that the reign of Babylon was already over, that the rule of Darius had begun, and Jeremiah's prophecy (29.10) was not fulfilled, he felt compelled to pray and ask God about it.

To seek by prayer: i.e. to seek *with prayer* by way of variation from *with fasting*, etc. He tells us that he prayed, fasting with sackcloth on his body, wallowing in ashes and prostrating himself upon them.

⁴I prayed to the LORD my God, making confession thus: "O Lord, great and awesome God, who stays faithful to His covenant with those who love Him and keep His commandments!

4. Observe here **prayer** and **confession** in contrast with *prayer and supplications* of ver. 3. The prayer contains four subjects: (a) Glorification of God: ver. 4b. (b) Enumeration of sins and offences: verses 5-11 a. (c) Enumeration of Israel's sufferings in consequence of their sins: verses 11 b-14. (d) Petition that God would turn from his wrath against the city and the nation: and that he would forgive their sins. The word *prayer* is made to include *all four* subjects (ver. 21), or *three* only, but differently. In ver. 2 it refers to the three first. In ver. 4, it excludes the confession of sin, and includes the remaining three. He prefaces the prayer with a record of the work of God, as is the custom with those who ask God for anything they desire: cp. Deuteronomy 3.24.

In this preface three qualities are mentioned: (a) **great**: i.e. the Doer of surprising things, which none except He can do; (b) **dreadful**: meaning that He is feared when He takes vengeance upon His enemies, so that they tremble; (c) **who keeps covenant and mercy**: indicating that He had fulfilled the covenant, i.e. the promises He had made to the patriarchs; and the **mercy**, i.e. the promises given on Mount Sinai, and the covenant of the plains of Moab. This is called mercy because it was an *extension* of the former. The **great and terrible** will then refer to the miracles created by Him in Egypt, the Wilderness, and in the Land itself, whereby He fulfilled all His promises to the patriarchs.

137

⁵We have sinned; we have gone astray; we have acted wickedly; we have been rebellious and have deviated from Your commandments and Your rules, ⁶and have not obeyed Your servants the prophets who spoke in Your name to our kings, our officers, our fathers, and all the people of the land.

5. **We have sinned**: Psalms 106.36, etc.; with reference to the seven nations.

And have dealt perversely: with reference to *abominations,* unlawful marriages, etc.

And have done wickedly: with reference to *injuries,* such as theft, oppression, etc.

And have rebelled: with reference to the slaying, beating, and imprisoning of the prophets.

And turned aside from your precepts: i.e. rules concerning Sabbath, feast-days, etc.

And judgments: referring to iniquitous verdicts.

6. We have not received their address to us: 'Return from your evil ways!' **And to all the people of the land** (after our fathers). Either our fathers are the elders and the people of authority, and the people of the land the subjects; or the latter may be the Gentiles.

In ver. 5 he mentioned their neglect of God's commandments in each particular; here he observes that they would not receive his warnings.

⁷With You, O Lord, is the right, and the shame is on us to this very day, on the men of Judah and the inhabitants of Jerusalem, all Israel, near and far, in all the lands where You have banished them, for the trespass they committed against You. ⁸The shame, O LORD, is on us, on our kings, our officers, and our fathers, because we have sinned against You.

7. **LORD, righteousness belongs to You**: i.e. Your cause against us is clear. If You have not dealt kindly with us; we are ashamed, seeing that we have neglected Your worship and served what has no right to service (cf. Jeremiah 11.26). They were ashamed before the nations of the world; when they witnessed the filthiness of their deeds (Jeremiah 6.15).

To the men of Judah, and to the inhabitants of Jerusalem: in this verse the whole nation is spoken of collectively. He mentions first the kingdom of Judah (the more honorable), and then the kingdom of Israel. This is according to the custom of the Bible in several books, which is to name Judah before Israel. Perhaps, however, it is put here first because the shame of Judah is greater than that of Israel (Ezekiel 15.51).

Who are near and who are far off: i.e. from the land (cp. Deuteronomy 13.7). Or, those carried away captive a short time after and those carried away captive a long time ago, sc. the ten tribes.

Because of their transgression which they have committed against You: 'they have transgressed Your covenants,' because they swore to God and made a covenant with Him, and then broke it (Jeremiah 5. 11, 11.10).

8. **To us belongs confusion of face** is repeated. The first perhaps refers to the multitude the second to the court; compare the rest of the verse. Our fathers will then refer to the Judges and Elders (Ezekiel 8.11). It may be repeated merely in order to contrast their actions with those of God.

139

⁹To the Lord our God belong mercy and forgiveness, for we rebelled against Him, ¹⁰and did not obey the LORD our God by following His teachings that He set before us through His servants the prophets. ¹¹All Israel has violated Your teaching and gone astray, disobeying You; so the curse and the oath written in the Teaching of Moses, the servant of God, have been poured down upon us, for we have sinned against Him.

9. Confusion, he says, is upon us for two reasons: (1) the magnitude of our sins and breach of the covenant; (2) because, in spite of our evil actions, God has spared us and had mercy on us, and forgiven us (cp. Ezekiel 56.61, 62).

Mercies and forgivenesses: mercies meaning that He spared them in the time of His anger (2 Kings 13.23); and forgivenesses at the time of their repentance (Nehemiah 9.17). These were their relations with Him while they were in the Land. As for the time of the Captivity, His mercies still rested upon them (Psalms 106.46; Lamentations 3.22).

Though we have rebelled against Him: i.e. in spite of all our offences, His mercy is upon us.

10. In ver. 6 he said *neither have we listened*, which he repeats here to finish the sentence; i.e. after saying **O LORD, to us belongs confusion of face**, and after that **to the LORD our God belong mercies and forgivenesses**. He goes on to say, 'although we have rebelled against Him' (meaning, as stated, that they had broken His covenant). He attaches to this the statement **neither have we listened to the voice of the LORD our God**; meaning the prophets came to us telling us to return to Your law. However, we did not listen to them, so that our sin doubled; *since first*, we violated the covenant, and *secondly*, we disobeyed Your prophets. This is the reason for the repetition.

By the hand of His servants the prophets: including all the prophets sent to us by God, those whose prophecies are recorded in writing, and all others; showing that the prophets urged us to walk in the laws of God.

140

In His laws (plural), specifically, a number of special laws; compare this to the phrase 'This is the law for the burnt-offering and meat-offering' of the sacrifices, etc.

All Israel: not all individual members of the nation, since there were among them prophets and saints; but *all the tribes of Israel,* since no one tribe was free from sin, such as idolatry, etc. As for the history of the Calf, we know indeed that the tribe of Levi, without exception, refused to worship the Calf (Exodus 32.26, where *Who?* means 'Of all the tribes of Israel, who does not worship the Calf, but only worships the LORD?' *and then joined themselves to him the whole tribe of Levi),* from which they earned their high dignity *(ibid.* 29). Otherwise there was not one of the tribes that did not worship idols, and commit deadly sins. It was done by their chiefs [and also by the common people] (Ezekiel 22.26; Jeremiah 11.8, 26). Therefore, he says all Israel have transgressed Your laws, meaning they have neglected their contents, and 'thrown them behind their backs' (Nehemiah 9.26; meaning 'have transgressed Your word by Your prophets'). This is repeated to make it clear that it was because Israel neglected the law and did not receive His word through His prophets that the curse recorded in His Book fell on them. The curse is the one mentioned in Deuteronomy 27.15; the oath is mentioned in the Chapter of the Covenant. All of it, he says, has fallen on Israel.

¹²He carried out the threat that He made against us, and against our rulers who ruled us, to bring upon us great misfortune; under the whole heaven there has never been done the like of what was done to Jerusalem. ¹³All that calamity, just as is written in the Teaching of Moses, came upon us, yet we did not supplicate the LORD our God, did not repent of our iniquity or become wise through Your truth. ¹⁴Hence the LORD was intent upon bringing calamity upon us, for the LORD our God is in the right in all that He has done, but we have not obeyed Him.

12. **He has confirmed His words**: i.e. the evils recorded as threatened by the prophets.

Against our judges that judged us: the kings and judges who were unrighteous, and ruined the nation; from whom destruction came on all.

For under the whole heaven has not been done, et cetera: i.e. their eating the flesh of parents and children, etc.

13. All that the prophets told, he says, is written in the law of Moses, the servant of God. God has formed a covenant with our forefathers on these terms. Therefore, He did not do any wrong to them. On the contrary, He spared them, though their sins deserved something far heavier (cp. Ezra 9.13). Nevertheless, in spite of their being visited by the afflictions mentioned, because of the extent of their sins, they had not returned to God and implored Him to turn from His wrath (Ezekiel 22.30).

And have discernment in Your truth: i.e. take into account the covenant You made with us, so that we might have abstained from such transgressions, thinking of the covenants and agreements whereby we were bound.

14. **Therefore has the LORD watched over the evil**: i.e. since they did not repent, He did not forgive or excuse them.

For the LORD our God is righteous in all His works: i.e. He was just in all that He brought upon them, though He did not do in any other nation of the world what He had done in Jerusalem.

142

And we have not obeyed His voice: i.e. the exiles. In spite of every disaster that came on us, and our falling into captivity, nevertheless they did not receive God's warning, or turn from their transgressions.

¹⁵"Now, O Lord our God—You who brought Your people out of the land of Egypt with a mighty hand, winning fame for Yourself to this very day—we have sinned, we have acted wickedly. ¹⁶O Lord, as befits Your abundant benevolence, let Your wrathful fury turn back from Your city Jerusalem, Your holy mountain; for because of our sins and the iniquities of our fathers, Jerusalem and Your people have become a mockery among all who are around us.
¹⁷"O our God, hear now the prayer of Your servant and his plea, and show Your favor to Your desolate sanctuary, for the Lord's sake.

15. So far for the enumeration of their sins and the recounting of the disasters and tribulations that had fallen on the nation. At the end of this he says: And now, O LORD, Who brought Your people out of Egypt by ten plagues, and have manifested their might and their superiority above the nations of the world, You have no nation except them, and we have repaid You by evil.'

16. **LORD, according to all Your mercies**: i.e. deal with us according to Your ancient custom, whereby You used to turn from Your wrath and have mercy upon us. The seventy years have passed, and the land has received her due for our neglect of sabbatical years and jubilees.

Let Your anger and Your fury be turned away: referring to the restoration of Israel there, that the land might be inhabited.

Your anger: the desolation of the Holy City; **Your wrath**: the burning of the Temple.

Connect for our sins with Jerusalem, and for the sins of our fathers with Your people. Both became a reproach; Jerusalem, as being burnt and lying desolate; Israel, through the disasters that had fallen on them, the Captivity, and their expulsion from their City. The City and the Nation are mentioned, because Daniel asked Almighty God for the City to be inhabited, and that Israel might return there out of

144

Captivity.

17. **The prayer of Your servant**: referring to the three portions enumerated above, *ad* ver. 4; and his supplications, ver. 16 to end.

And cause Your face to shine: of which the building of the city and its habitation will be the result.

For Your sake: for Your Name's sake, since You have called it My House. In the previous verse he spoke of the City and Nation, here he speaks of the Temple. He speaks of the City and Nation together, but of the Temple separately, because the City was inhabited by Israel, but the Temple was more important than the City.

¹⁸Incline Your ear, O my God, and hear; open Your eyes and see our desolation and the city to which Your name is attached. Not because of any merit of ours do we lay our plea before You but because of Your abundant mercies. ¹⁹O Lord, hear! O Lord, forgive! O Lord, listen, and act without delay for Your own sake, O my God; for Your name is attached to Your city and Your people!"
²⁰While I was speaking, praying, and confessing my sin and the sin of my people Israel, and laying my supplication before the LORD my God on behalf of the holy mountain of my God—

18. He returns to the City, mentioning the holy cities, which surrounded Jerusalem. 'O LORD,' he says, 'hear my petition, and see what has overtaken Your holy cities, which have become waste and burnt with fire. Re-people them with their inhabitants.'

Not for our own righteousness: indicating that others were praying besides Daniel. 'It is not by our merits or good deeds that we entreat You; for we have transgressed, and multiplied our sins. No, our confidence is in Your great mercy. Please have mercy on us and our cities.

19. This ends the prayer. **Hear**: i.e. hear our complaint concerning our condition and what has happened to us, and forgive our sins. **Listen**: i.e. listen to our request; and do sc. something for Your people, Your city, and Your temple.

For Your own sake: i.e. because Your Name is called upon Your city (cp. Jeremiah 25.29); and Your Name, too, is 'God of Israel.' So do for the sake of Your Name, and do not magnify our sins and transgressions.

20. **Speaking**: ver. 4. **Praying**: referring to the lamentations. **Confessing**: the seventeen phrases beginning with ver. 5 and ending with 16 a.

My sin and the sin of my people: Up to this point, he associated himself with the nation. Here, he mentions his sin separately. According to some, until Daniel grew up he had been educated in his parents' teaching; only when he could

146

think for himself had he thrown it off. According to others, he says my sin, because no son of Adam is free from sin, which some commit intentionally and others unintentionally (hence Ecclesiastes 7.20). Others still suppose he says this because it was impossible for him to express displeasure at evildoers, owing to the wicked having the upper hand.

²¹while I was uttering my prayer, the man Gabriel, whom I had previously seen in the vision, was sent forth in flight and reached me about the time of the evening offering. ²²He made me understand by speaking to me and saying, "Daniel, I have just come forth to give you understanding.

21. **Speaking in prayer** includes the whole prayer from ver. 4 to the end.

Whom I had seen in the vision at the beginning: 8.16, where another angel sent him to Daniel, and Daniel had become familiar with him. Gabriel is one of the special angels who stand before the Glory, having six wings with which they fly (Isaiah 6.2).

Wearily: i.e. quickly.

Touched me about the time of the evening offering: at evening; some say *before* the regular prayer, others *after* it. Most probably the latter view is right, viz. he first offered up the regular prayer, and followed it with the foregoing petition.

The evening offering: i.e. the evening *burnt offering;* the word hHnm means simply 'offering' (Genesis 4.4; Psalms 141.2).

22. **He instructed me and talked with me**: *v. infra.*

I am now come forth: from before the Glory; and have been sent to instruct you in what you need to know, and you will instruct Israel.

²³A word went forth as you began your plea, and I have come to tell it, for you are precious; so mark the word and understand the vision.
²⁴"Seventy weeks[a] have been decreed for your people and your holy city until the measure of transgression is filled and that of sin complete, until iniquity is expiated, and eternal righteousness ushered in; and prophetic vision ratified,[b] and the Holy of Holies anointed.

23. **At the beginning**: from the moment when you began to say 'O LORD' (ver. 16), the answer came, 'and I have come to instruct you in what I have been commanded to instruct you.' Observe that he does not say 'at the beginning of your prayer.' Apparently, while Daniel was recounting their sins, and what had befallen Israel, He was listening. However, when he began to say, 'LORD, according to all Your righteousness,' the answer arrived, and Gabriel came to him. This is the treatment of those who are perfect with their Creator: 'before they cry He answers' (Isaiah 42.24). To those who are not perfect in His eyes He delays the answer ten days; as was the case with Johanan the son of Kareah (Jeremiah 42.8, where the answer was not delayed on Jeremiah's account, but only on account of the people).

For you are a man of desires: 'since you *desire* to know the fate of the Temple and of the Nation.'

Consider the matter, and understand the vision: i.e. all the previous words that he had heard from the angels in the Dream and the Vision. Some of these he explains in this chapter; *v. infra*. The words may be taken either as infinitives or as imperatives without difference to the meaning.

24. He tells him what is going to happen during the **four kingdoms**. Of these *seventy weeks*, *seven* passed in the kingdom of the Chaldees (47 years); 57 years the Persians reigned, 180

---

[a] *Viz., of years.*
[b] *Lit. "sealed."*

the Greeks, 206 the Romans. These are the special periods of the seventy weeks. These include the reigns of all four beasts. The angel does not describe at length what happened to any of them except the history of the Second Temple during the time of Rome. These seventy weeks are *weeks of sabbatical years*, making 490 years; below they are divided into periods.

Are decreed upon your people: decreed by God, like the 400 years decreed to Abraham, or the 70 years decreed to Babylon.

Upon your people and upon your holy place: in so far as different sorts of fortune befell the people during this period, some commendable and others to be condemned. Six things are mentioned in this verse, three commendable, **to finish transgression, to make an end of sins, to make reconciliation for iniquity**; and three are mentioned of a different aspect, **to bring in everlasting righteousness, to seal up vision and prophecy, and to anoint the most holy**. Of these six, some are to take place at the beginning of the series, others at the end of 300 years. **To bring everlasting righteousness and to anoint the most holy** refers to the first beginning of the building of the Temple. To seal up vision and prophecy took place during the reign of *the Greeks*. **to finish transgression** etc. was done in the middle of the 70 years of Babylon.

Transgression refers to the 'worship of other gods' and similar 'abominations,' sins, to the misplacing of the Sabbaths and the other feasts. Iniquity includes the other sins committed by the people among themselves, i.e. offences against life and property or possessions. Others interpret this differently; referring to 'make reconciliation for iniquity' to 'offerings:' meaning that while they were in Babylon, to the end of the Babylonian empire, God was compensated for the debt Israel had incurred from their sins: referring to 2 Chronicles 36.21.

150

Similarly, **to bring in everlasting righteousness** is supposed by some to refer to the High Priests, and **to anoint the most holy** to the sanctuaries and the priests. Others again make **everlasting righteousness** the offerings, and the most holy the High Priest, referring to 2 Chronicles 33. 13. Either way it must plainly take place at the building of the Temple. There remains **to seal up vision and prophecy**: this must mean the cutting off of vision and prophets from Israel. **Vision** refers to prophecies relating to the future, such as those of Haggai or Zechariah of the future; and **the prophet** (i.e. prophecy) is what is told relating to the present. According to some authorities the Holy Spirit was cut off from the time of Solomon; the *Singers* remaining, who recited the Psalms (see 2 Chronicles 29. 20). Or again he may mean by **to seal up vision and prophecy** that the Books of the Prophets were sealed and collected, twenty-four books, and fixed by *Massorahs,* and other institutions necessary for this purpose. He puts **to seal vision and prophecy** between **to bring everlasting righteousness** and **to anoint the most holy** because prophecy went on between the offering of the oblations and the anointing of the most holy.

²⁵You must know and understand: From the issuance of the word to restore and rebuild Jerusalem until the [time of the] anointed leader is seven weeks; and for sixty-two weeks it will be rebuilt, square and moat, but in a time of distress.

25. **From the going forth of the commandment**: supposed to refer to Jeremiah 29.10, or to *going forth* from God; to return: i.e. the captives with the sacred vessels; **to the anointed one, the Khalif**: i.e. the High Priest, who is *anointed* with the 'oil of anointing,' and is *the prince* of the LORD's house. Others make **the anointed** the High Priest, and the prince Zerubbabel son of Shealtiel. He tells him then that from the time of the destruction of the Holy Place and the captivity of the nation to the building of the Second Temple, is *seven weeks,* i.e. forty-nine years. Now the people did not cease dwelling in the city until the twenty-third year of Nebuchadnezzar; they are called (Ezekiel 33.24) 'inhabitants of waste places,' and were taken captive by Nebuzaradan (Jeremiah 52.30). Now if twenty-three years is taken away from the sum total of the seventy years of Babylon, there remain forty-seven years, plus one year for Darius and one year for Cyrus. This makes a total of forty-nine years; to which the *seven weeks* refer.

Seven weeks, and sixty-two weeks it will be built again: this is the duration of the Second Temple until the coming of TITUS THE SINNER, king of Rome; 434 years.

During this period, he tells Daniel, Jerusalem will again be inhabited.

Market-place: i.e. the forum of the judges.

Decision: i.e. the performance of legal sentences of death, etc.

The dough of the times[2]: referring, it is said, to the offering of the High Priest (Leviticus 6.13). **Of the times**:

---

[2]Mistranslation for ' even in troublous times.'

152

inasmuch as half was offered in the morning, and half in the evening.

The offering of the High Priest is mentioned separately, because so long as it was offered the altar continued in service.

²⁶And after those sixty-two weeks, the anointed one will disappear and vanish.ᶜ The army of a leader who is to come will destroy the city and the sanctuary, but its end will come through a flood. Desolation is decreed until the end of war. ²⁷During one week he will make a firm covenant with many. For half a week he will put a stop to the sacrifice and the meal offering. At the ᶜ⁻ corner [of the altar]ᶜ will be an appalling abomination until the decreed destruction will be poured down upon the appalling thing."

26. **And after the sixty-two weeks**: at the close of these sixty-two weeks this Anointed, spoken of in ver. 25, will be cut off; referring to the cessation of priests from the altar.

And will have nothing: i.e. no son or successor in his place; *or*, the whole time of the Captivity they will have no royalty.

The city and the sanctuary: Jerusalem, and the Temple of the LORD.

Will destroy: will devastate and burn (Psalms 137.7).

The people of the prince that will come: the army of Rome with Titus.

And his end will be with a flood: i.e. those that are left of Israel after the massacre will be *swept away*, i.e. carried away captive. This is the description of what happened to the sanctuary, Jerusalem, and the nation.

To the end of war: i.e. until the end of wars, sc. the *wars of Gog*, Jerusalem and the cities of Judah will lie waste; as has been witnessed up to our day.

27. One week is left out of the seventy; he describes their condition therein. The enemy, he says, made a covenant with them for seven years, stating that he would not carry them away captive or harm them. When half the week had passed,

---

ᶜ *Meaning of Heb. uncertain*
ᶜ⁻ *Meaning of Heb. uncertain*
⁻ᶜ *Meaning of Heb. uncertain*

he betrayed them, and broke the covenant. Some suppose that what induced him to do this was that he saw the people withdrew from the city in detachments, observing that they must certainly otherwise be taken captive or fall before the enemy. They said, 'Let us withdraw of our own accord: it is better.' Some say that the Israelites killed certain Gentiles that were in the city, who were Roman nobles. When they had done this, the Romans broke faith with them, took the city, burnt the Temple, and put a stop to the offerings (he will cause the sacrifice and the offering to cease). The histories further tell us that he set up in God's house an idol, and offered up swine on God's altar.

The wing of abominations: the army of the Romans, who are called 'abominations;' they are the devastators of the sanctuary (one that makes desolate).

Even to the consummation and the determination: i.e. until God work a *consummation* and a *determination* by causing the nations to cease, and especially Edom. The first referring to the city [of Rome]; the second to the kingdom.

Will be poured out upon the wasted: i.e. the wrath of God upon this city, which will be waste until Israel comes and inhabit it. God showed this to Daniel because he wanted to know what would become of the people and the Holy Place in the time of the three kingdoms. He knew that the Holy Place *must* one day be inhabited, and the captives *must* return. However, they *might* have continued in the conditions in which they lived during the time of the Persian and Greek empires. God showed him that the city must again be destroyed, and the people taken captive, so he and Israel would know it. From this, his heart was pained, and he sickened.

155

X

In the third year of King Cyrus of Persia, an oracle was revealed to Daniel, who was called Belteshazzar. That oracle was true, [a]but it was a great task to understand the prophecy; understanding came to him through the vision.[-a]

X.

1. In the third year of Cyrus, he tells us, an angel appeared to him, who told him all that God would reveal to him. This is *the fourth section*. The same thing happened twice in the reign of Belshazzar, and once in the reign of Darius. This is the fourth time. Apparently, until the first year of the reign of Cyrus he was engaged in the Sultan's business; see on chap. 1. *ult.* Then, he withdrew from it, having received leave, especially after the proclamation (Ezra 1.3). Then again he had become old, and his heart was affected by what he had been told of the future capture of the city and the return of the nation into captivity, as was explained before. Then he began to lament and fast, in order to ask God about what was on his mind. He sought help for his request in lamentation as before, chap. 9

A thing was revealed: i.e. a matter that was difficult, and whose interpretation was hidden from him, became clear after being obscure.

And the thing was true: i.e. *Literally* true, not like the Dream or the Vision, see on 9.26. Notice that this word *true* occurs four times, with the same meaning; 9.26 is the first, the present passage the second; 10.21 and 9.2.

Whose name was called Belteshazzar: not ' *whose name was B.*' Some think the name still remained upon him, and that he did not get rid of it. Others infer that he was called by that

---

[a-] *Meaning of Heb. uncertain*
[-a] *Meaning of Heb. uncertain*

name until the fall of the Chaldean empire, and that the appellation ceased with its end; which is probable.

And a great host: i.e. the prophecy of a great host, whether *Edom* or *Ishmael* (see on 11.3).

And he understood the thing, etc.: i.e. the explanation of the communication made to him in the last chapter; and that of the *Vision* which he saw, i.e. chap. 8. See on the following verses.

²At that time, I, Daniel, kept three full weeks of mourning. ³I ate no tasty food, nor did any meat or wine enter my mouth. I did not anoint myself until the three weeks were over.

2, 3. **In those days**: in the third year of Cyrus; the same *days* in which he lamented. The phrase three weeks of days indicates the difference between these weeks and the seventy weeks; which were *of years*.

I was mourning: he mentions certain things which he practiced during those weeks; [in reference to] (1) food; (2) drink; (3) scent. Of food he mentions **bread** and **meat**; of drink **wine**. The *bread* he specifies as **pleasant**, since doubtless he must have eaten *some* bread. He explains that he did not eat fine wheat bread, especially. Of *meat and wine*, however, he says it *came not into my mouth*, since he did not eat or drink either. Probably, he ate *bread* made of barley or coarse wheat with a relish of vegetables and grain; and perhaps *fruit*. Next, he speaks of *oil* and *scent*, **neither did I anoint myself at all**. We know, too, that he must certainly have changed his clothing, put on rough garments, and shunned all entertainment. All this is what mourners normally do. It remains to speak of the *fasting*. Some say that he fasted [in order to gain knowledge], as the angel says, *infra* ver. 10: supposing that fasting is one form of mourning, which is not improbable; so that he bound himself to continue mourning until God would reveal to him what He would do about the affairs of the nation. This is similar to the mourning which David enforced on himself until God revealed to him His will; Psalms 132.3. The saints of God could do this, knowing that God would answer their request favorably. The people of the Captivity cannot venture so far, but can only stand up and ask God about such things as people like them can ask. We must explain the nature of the meat Daniel abstained from eating. Let us state that it refers to *meat which was lawful to eat*, since he only abstained during these days from the four

158

things which in previous times he had been accustomed to. He returned to these things after the revelation of what God revealed to him. As to food which had always been unlawful for him to eat, that cannot be included in the terms of the verse; nor can the word *treat* refer to the flesh of forbidden beasts, birds, and fish. Nor again to the flesh of oxen and sheep, which is only lawful after the performance of the conditions contained in the laws, as we have explained in the Commentary on the Pentateuch and the Book of Commandments which we have compiled. If any one ignorant of Hebrew should ask, 'What flesh is that?' we answer, the meat of birds, land animals, and fish. If he asks again, 'How can you show that rWb in Hebrew means "fish"?' We answer, 'rWb is a name for both birds and fish, nor is there any distinction between fish and other animals.' However, we can prove it by a text: Num. 11.21, 'You have said, I will give them flesh;' 22, Will flocks and herds be slain for them? Or will all the fish of the sea be gathered together for them?' This shows that 'fish' are 'flesh' (rWb), no less than oxen and sheep. Then birds are called so in the same chapter; ver. 33, 'While the flesh (i.e. the quails) was yet between their teeth.' Similarly birds are coupled with beasts in Leviticus 17.13, 14; and the same is indicated in the history of Noah. It is clear then that rWb is a name for *every* animal beyond question. Those who allow meat during the Captivity, then, cannot use this verse as evidence, especially as the altar of God was being employed, and sacrifices continually offered on it; for it had now been built a whole year.

⁴It was on the twenty-fourth day of the first month, when I was on the bank of the great river—the Tigris—⁵that I looked and saw a man dressed in linen, his loins girt in ^{b-}fine gold.^{-b} ⁶His body was like beryl, his face had the appearance of lightning, his eyes were like flaming torches, his arms and legs had the color of burnished bronze, and the sound of his speech was like the noise of a multitude.

4. This verse indicates that it was after the conclusion of the three weeks. So we learn that he began to lament on the third of the month. He tells us that he was walking on the bank of the Tigris, when this angel appeared to him. Observe that in the Vision he was not in reality on the bank of the river Ulai. He only saw this in a Vision, whereas he saw this when he was awake, when he was standing in reality on the river's bank. He does not say at what point on the bank he was-Mosul, Babylon, or elsewhere. The source of the Tigris is above Mosul, and it flows into the Marshes.

5. **Uphaz** is the name of a place (Jeremiah 10.9).

6. This angel is not Gabriel, as some have thought, since he was already familiar with Gabriel; nor was his form so mighty and terrible. On the contrary, when he saw him at the end of his prayer he was not affected in this way at all, as we will explain. Nor does he describe any of the angels whom he mentions as he describes this angel, because to his fear and terror of him. We will state what is necessary on this subject on ver. 13.

Then he describes the color of his body: from his neck to his knees it resembled the color of the blue stone. His face, he says, was like flashing lightning; and its color red like lightning. And his eyes, he said, were like torches of fire that sparkle to a distance. His arms and legs, he tells us, were like the color of burnished brass, i.e. yellow. And his voice was

---

^{b-} *Or "gold of Uphaz."*
^{-b} *Or "gold of Uphaz."*

heard at a distance like the **noise of an army**. All these things would frighten the observer. His garments were those **of authority**, girt up after the fashion of a warrior whose garments are tied in the middle. He had come to him from battle: v. *infra*.

⁷I, Daniel, alone saw the vision; the men who were with me did not see the vision, yet they were seized with a great terror and fled into hiding. ⁸So I was left alone to see this great vision. I was drained of strength, my vigor was destroyed, and I could not summon up strength. ⁹I heard him speaking; and when I heard him speaking, overcome by a deep sleep, I lay prostrate on the ground. ¹⁰Then a hand touched me, and shook me onto my hands and knees.

7. Observe that he did not see the angel on the bank, but only in the air, above the river, raised above its surface, cp. 52.6; and he tells us that he saw him in this terrible, frightening form.

For the men who were with me: indicating that there were people with him, and that he saw, but no one else. Now the words **I alone saw the Vision** already tell us that he alone saw it: what then is the purpose of the clause **For the men that were with me...** ? Answer: to indicate that these people, although they did not *see*, yet felt something, and began **quaking**; which was possibly caused by the sound of his voice. They heard the sound, but did not see the figure. **They did not see the Vision**; not, 'they did not hear.' On the contrary, when they did hear his voice, they began trembling, and fled scared. Probably these were people who had gone out with him for some purpose not mentioned by the Scripture. Similarly when our forefathers heard the voice of God they felt fear and began trembling, and they fled far off (Exodus 20.18).

8. In the previous verse he said, 'And I Daniel alone saw the Vision;' in the present, **So I was left alone**; and there was none with me to keep me company.

There remained no strength in me: to stand.

And I retained no strength: to move.

My comeliness was turned in me into corruption: i.e., 'his face became yellow, as happens to people at the time of death.

162

9. **I was fallen into a deep sleep**: he had swooned for a little.

10. **A hand**: i.e. the angel's hand, whose hand he saw, but not the angel moving it, so that he rose up from being on his face, and was on all fours; not having strength to sit down or to stand.

¹¹He said to me, "O Daniel, precious man, mark what I say to you and stand up, for I have been sent to you." After he said this to me, I stood up, trembling. ¹²He then said to me, "Have no fear, Daniel, for from the first day that you set your mind to get understanding, practicing abstinence before your God, your prayer was heard, and I have come because of your prayer. ¹³However, the prince of the Persian kingdom opposed me for twenty-one days; now Michael, a prince of the first rank, has come to my aid, after I was detained there with the kings of Persia. ¹⁴So I have come to make you understand what is to befall your people in the days to come, for there is yet a vision for those days."
¹⁵While he was saying these things to me, I looked down and kept silent.

11. He commanded him to do two things: first, to listen to what he would say to him, telling him that God had sent him; secondly, to stand on his feet, so he would hear his voice. And he tells us that he did stand, yet not firmly, but was trembling.

12. **Don't be afraid**: Do not fear that your station in God's eyes may have been lowered, seeing that before when you prayed the answer came to you while you was praying, and this time three weeks have passed and you have not received an answer. No. On the first day that you prayed, your words were heard, only I had a task that prevented me from coming to you.

Your words were heard indicates that he was also asking God to instruct him; and he adds that he came to tell him what God thought important to tell him.

13-15. What prevented him from coming on the first day, he says, was his fighting with the Prince of Persia. The idea is that he fought with him until Cyrus died. When Cyrus died he left and came to Daniel. We will supplement this so far as is necessary at 11.1. As soon, he adds, as I had finished fighting with the Prince of Persia, I came to tell you what will happen to your people at the latter time; i.e. the time of the

164

end of the four kingdoms.

For the Vision is yet for many days: i.e. the vision that you saw before relates to the latter time, i.e. to the end of the four kingdoms.

When the angel had proceeded to this point, Daniel's terror overpowered him, and he had no strength to stand, but fell on his face.

And I was dumb: there was no strength left in him to speak to the angel about what he said. He became dumb and could not talk at all.

¹⁶Then one who looked like a man touched my lips, and I opened my mouth and spoke, saying to him who stood before me, "My lord, because of the vision, I have been seized with pangs and cannot summon strength. ¹⁷How can this servant of my lord speak with my lord, seeing that my strength has failed and no spirit is left in me?" ¹⁸He who looked like a man touched me again, and strengthened me. ¹⁹He said, "Have no fear, precious man, all will be well with you; be strong, be strong!" As he spoke with me, I was strengthened, and said, "Speak on, my lord, for you have strengthened me!"

16, 17. He saw an angel, resembling a man, talking with him; perhaps the angel's hand approached his mouth; cp. Isaiah 6.6; Jeremiah 1.9 - When the angel had approached him, his mouth was opened and, he spoke.

To him who stood before me: the great angel who had addressed him. He said this as an excuse: 'If it hadn't been for the fright that came over me, and my strength failing, I would have stood up as you told me.'

My sorrows are turned upon me: cp. 1 Sam. 3.19.

For how can, etc.? i.e. I have no power to stand up to speak with such as my LORD. My rank is not so high.

Immediately: since I met you, I cannot move, and my strength has left me. Perhaps breath here means *reason* so Job 26.4; 32.8.

18. When the hand touched him he spoke; but there was no strength in him to stand. So, the angel repeated what he had done, and approached him. Then, he found strength to stand. The great angel was above the river: Daniel at first saw his hand, but nothing more. Afterwards, he saw himself; and the angel talked with him informally. Then, he touched Daniel's lips, and approached him. Possibly, the angel took his hand and drew him up: **strengthened** him.

19. **Don't be afraid**: spoken by the great angel; meaning Do not fear for yourself. Rise up at once; be comforted, strengthen your heart, and hear what I will tell you.' When he

166

had heard his voice, his heart was strengthened, he having
stood upon his feet beforehand.

²⁰Then he said, "Do you know why I have come to you? Now I must go back to fight the prince of Persia. When I go off, the prince of Greece will come in. ²¹ᶜˉNo one is helping me against them except your prince, Michael. However, I will tell you what is recorded in the book of truth.ˉᶜ

20. **Do you know?** referring to his previous words (ver. 12). 'I have told you already,' he says, ' why I am come; and I must immediately return to fight with the Prince of Persia concerning the four kings which are left to Persia.' This is explained in what fellows.

When I go forth: i.e. I will go forth from fighting with the Prince of Persia, and afterwards the Prince of Greece will come. He does not tell what will come after Greece.

21. **That which is inscribed in the writing of truth**: i.e. that which he had heard in the Dream he wrote down (7.1). 'This,' he says, 'which is inscribed in the writing of truth has an inner meaning, which I will develop for you without further allegory.'

There is none who holds with me against these: No one helped me to destroy these kingdoms except Michael.

Your prince: indicating that Michael is Prince of Israel, and that the angel conversing with him was demolishing the kingdoms with Michael.

Against these: either, the kings of Persia, who have just been mentioned; or, the four kingdoms. These two angels were helping each other to put an end to all these kingdoms. The great angel does not state that he is prince of any one of the dominions. Perhaps Michael fought with the enemies of Israel only; and this one with the ruler of every nation, whom he deposed, when the period of its influence was over.

XI

"In the first year of Darius the Mede, I took my stand to strengthen and fortify him.

XI.

1. Just as he had helped Michael to kill Cyrus, so he had helped him to slay Darius, or had killed him. Here we must pause a moment and briefly state some necessary ideas on the subject of angels. We are not justified in setting aside the literal meaning of the Word of God or of His prophets, except where that literal meaning is hindered or precluded because it is contradicted by *reason* or by *a clear text*. In such a case it is understood that the first text requires an explanation reconciling it with reason or with the other text; the words having been used in some metaphorical or improper sense, as we have observed in a number of places in the Law and the Blessed Prophets. Ideas repudiated by *reason,* are such as 'God descended,' 'God ascended,' etc.; are prohibited by reason, because, if we take the verse literally, it follows from it that God must be material: capable of inhabiting places and being in one place more than in another, moving and resting; these are all qualities of created and finite beings; and He must possess these attributes. Such texts must therefore be capable of being explained, and the term indirectly interpreted may be either the *noun* or the *verb*. The first, the noun, is done in cases like 'and God descended,' 'and God ascended,' where we affirm the action of the person of whom 'ascending' and 'descending' are attributes. However, the person intended is the *Angel* of God, or the *Glory* of God, or the *Messenger of* God, with the ellipse of a word. The second, the verb, is done in cases like 'God was glad,' or 'God was sorry,' or 'God was jealous;' all of which are accidents not to be predicated of the Immortal Creator. This phrase must contain a sense to be

169

developed in whatever way the words will allow. In such cases as these, the language has employed metaphors and inaccurate expressions; the application of the reason can point them out. Where one text is excluded by another, the one that allows two or more interpretations must be explained.

Now, no clear text of Scripture denies the possibility of God's having created angels; nor does the reason reject it. Neither can their existence be rejected, whether we hold they are accidents, or that they are created and destroyed. Angels are mentioned in the Scriptures in many places, in two different ways. Sometimes they appear sensibly and are witnessed by people, like any other visible object; sometimes they appear in dreams, and there too like other objects. Instances of the first type of appearance were witnessed by Jacob, Moses, Balaam, Joshua, Gideon, Manoah, David, Nebuchadnezzar, and Daniel. Instances of the second type of appearance were witnessed by Abimelech (as some think), Jacob, and Balaam. Their voices too have been heard without their being seen, as by Hagar, Abraham, Samuel, and David. These all occur in our Chronicles, and there is no ground for rejecting these texts. It is known that nothing but *body* can be perceived by the sense of the eye: and that an accident cannot exist by itself. An angel therefore must have a *body*. Now, a body cannot bring itself into existence. It must have a Creator to create it. Furthermore, it is a thing which persists. An angel, therefore, being created must be capable of persistence; and what is there to necessitate his annihilation?

If any one holds that an angel is only created for the moment, for the sake of a message or something similar, and when it is finished, there is no reason why he should endure - what, we ask, indicates that he is created at the moment - or created merely for the message or purpose which renders him for the moment necessary? If you say: 'Then what has the

170

angel to do besides delivering messages and similar tasks?' We answer: To praise and glorify his Creator. Is not the prophet too chosen to deliver a message? Nevertheless, he is not created merely to speak [and then be destroyed]. We find, in fact, in our accounts that angels *do* endure. Thus the Glory abode with the children of Israel nine hundred years. Daniel says of Gabriel, *and the man Gabriel, whom I had seen in the Vision at the beginning,* and a year had elapsed between the two occasions. Nor can we suppose the second Gabriel was merely like the first, who had been created a year before and then destroyed. That would not entitle the second to be [called] the same as the first. Again, there are the words of this angel who is speaking to Daniel, who says: 'I have been some time in war, and am going to fight those who remain:' see also 52.1. These verses point to their persistence. After this discussion there may be a stop put to the assertions of those who maintain that they are created for a moment and annihilated. As for their orders, doubtless some are higher than others; see our Commentary on Ezekiel, chap. 1, and Psalms 106.1.

Observe, too, that in this chapter Daniel says of one **like the similitude of a man**, and tells us that he came near him, and was not afraid, whereas he was terrified and alarmed by the *great angel.* Such things are common in our books; and their powers are limited according as the Creator has given them. Observe that when Jacob wrestled with the angel, the angel was unable to get rid of him (Genesis 32.26). Though their forms are frightening, God has given men the ability to see them, except the great and mighty Glory which the blessed Messenger [Moses] asked God to show him, when He said 'you can not,' etc. (Exodus 33.20). This is a concise account of this matter. We would gladly explain what we have said on this subject in other places. It would not, however, be proper to introduce that subject in this place.

171

I stood up to confirm: the province is Michael's, wherein this angel helped him.

²And now I will tell you the truth: Persia will have three more kings, and the fourth will be wealthier than them all; by the power he obtains through his wealth, he will stir everyone up against the kingdom of Greece. ³Then a warrior king will appear who will have an extensive dominion and do as he pleases. ⁴But after his appearance, his kingdom will be broken up and scattered to the four winds of heaven, but not for any of his posterity, nor with dominion like that which he had; for his kingdom will be uprooted and belong to others beside these.

2. *After Cyrus came four kings*: sc. Ahasuerus (Mordecai's patron), Artaxerxes the Less, Darius the Persian; these are the *three*.

And the fourth: i.e. Artaxerxes, patron of Ezra and Nehemiah.

Will be far richer: he already told us that Cyrus got the treasures of the kings, and was exceedingly rich (Isaiah 45.3); and the same wealth is asserted of Artaxerxes in Esther 1.4. In this verse he tells us that Artaxerxes was richer than all the Persian kings, and that he lived in his kingdom longer than the others, seeing that he reigned thirty-three years. Then he tells him that when he reaches the height of his wealth, his kingdom will end, and all will go to the king of Javan: he will stir up all. This was not told in the *Dream* or in the *Vision*, but only here.

3. **And there will stand up**: i.e. will be established on the throne.

A mighty king: the one called in the dream 'a notable horn between his eyes:' i.e. Alexander; called *mighty* because he took great cities. His history is well known.

Who will rule: the Persians ruled three quarters, see on chap. 8.4 etc., but Alexander all four (11.39).

And will do according to his will: cp. ver. 19, of Nebuchadnezzar.

4. **His kingdom will be broken**: the government was disturbed on Alexander's death. **and will be divided**: with

reference to the dispute between his generals, and the compromise that dictated each of the princes was to take one quarter of the globe. This was because he left no son (and not for his posterity).

Neither like to his government: in spite of these four holding the four quarters of the globe, they had no royal control or might like Alexander's.

For his kingdom will be broken: the kingdom of the Greeks, who owned the four quarters of the globe, will be shattered. Dynasty after dynasty will spring up on the death of these four, until 180 years have passed, according to the historical records.

And to others besides these: meaning that there arose after these a dynasty which discarded the traditions of its predecessors. These have been already mentioned in the words 'when sin is completed.' They were *sinners*, i.e. apostates, in respect of the traditions, [and usurpers] in respect of the government.

⁵"The king of the south will grow powerful; however, one of his officers will overpower him and rule, having an extensive dominion. ⁶After some years, an alliance will be made, and the daughter of the king of the south will come to the king of the north to effect the agreement, but she will not maintain her strength, nor will his strength endure. She will be surrendered together with those who escorted her and the one who begot her and helped her during those times.

5. Observe that the kingdom was divided between four, each one taking a quarter, like those who were mentioned above. This is seen from the expressions *king of the north, king of the south* (which we will clearly explain lower down). None of the four are mentioned, however, except the king of the *north* and the king of the *south*. Probably, therefore, the kings of the *west* and of the *east* remained quietly in their respective quarters, not seeking to acquire any other, and there was no war between them. Consequently, the Scripture does not mention them; whereas it mentions the kings of the *south* and of the *north*, because they were engaged in eventful wars. Or, possibly, the kings of the west and east were dependant, respectively, on the other two kings.

And of his princes: said to be one of the *princes* of the king who preceded him; the *king of the south* who preceded him being a Greek, and this one of the (latter's) princes. Otherwise, he is one of the princes of the *king of the north*, who gathered strength and rebelled against the king of the north, which is likely, and is confirmed by the following verse.

He will be strong above him: the king of the **south** above the king of the **north**.

A great dominion: his realm will be greater and wider than that of any other monarch; he being, in fact, the king of *Rome* (who is the king of the south), and this the first king who arose over them.

6. **At the end of years**: he does not say how many. This

175

refers to years during which there was an understanding between the two; until the king of the north rebelled against the king of the south. Because of this, the king of the south sent armies to the king of the north. It is like what happened to Sodom with Khedorlaomer, when they obeyed him for twelve years, then rebelled, and were attacked by him.

Will join themselves together: for battle; cp. Genesis 14.3.

And the daughter of the king of the south: i.e. the whole of his host; compare the phrases 'Daughter of Egypt,' 'Daughter of Tyre,' etc.

To make an agreement: i.e. to desire him to deal peacefully with him again and continue in his previous allegiance. This is like what Sennacheriv, king of Asshur, demanded of Hezekiah. Possibly, he wanted him to confess the former's faith, the king of the north being an idolater. The king of the north, though, would not agree to this, but came out to fight the army of the king of the south; and the army of the king of the south could not stand before the king of the north (**but she will not retain the strength of her arm**).

The arm is the **armies of the king of the south**, which will flee before the king of the north, and afterwards surrender (**but she will be given up**, etc.).

She will be given up refers to the army.

Those who brought her refers to the captains of the host.

He who begot her refers to the general of the army of the king of the south, who went with it; the king himself not going with it, on account of one of two possible circumstances. Either, he despised the king of the north, and was convinced that his army would rout him; or, perhaps, he was afraid that if he left his kingdom his affairs might become disturbed. Consequently, he did not leave from his place.

176

And he who strengthened her in those times: referring to certain people who were among his army who gave assistance, but did not actually belong. This refers to mercenaries; when they were required they went with his army, and afterwards returned to their homes.

⁷A shoot from her stock will appear in his place, will come against the army and enter the fortress of the king of the north; he will fight and overpower them. ⁸He will also take their gods with their molten images and their precious vessels of silver and gold back to Egypt as booty. For some years he will leave the king of the north alone,

7, 8. The king of the south had no power to face the king of the north, but died defeated. After his death there arose there another king in his stead.

Out of a shoot of her roots: this was not his son, but one of the royal seed related to him. This is a man of valor who took command of the army and went with it, fearing that what overtook the former might overtake his army.

And he will come to the army: i.e. the army which had surrendered to the king of the north. When they see he has arrived, they will return to him. Then, he will strengthen himself and will come to the fortified cities of the king of the north, especially the capital city.

And will deal with them: i.e. do battle with them, prevail against them, and kill some of them, i.e. the soldiers.

Next, he tells us how he will take their idols, out of spite against them. This is like what the king of Asshur did with the calves of Israel (Hosea 10.6).

With their princes: the king's lords and lieutenants.

The king did not fall into his hands, as some think -- because he fled, or because he sent messengers, and agreed to give him what the previous king desired, as we explained in ver. 6 b. This is most probable to my mind. Now the king of the south did not accept these terms from the king of the north until after he had taken their idols and all of their treasures. This was to rob him of his power, so the king of the north would be left very weak, and be compelled to absolute obedience to the king of the south.

⁹who will [later] invade the realm of the king of the south, but will go back to his land.
¹⁰"His sons will wage war, collecting a multitude of great armies; he will advance and sweep through as a flood, and will again wage war as far as his stronghold. ¹¹Then the king of the south, in a rage, will go out to do battle with him, with the king of the north. He will muster a great multitude, but the multitude will be delivered into his [foe's] power. ¹²But when the multitude is carried off, he will grow arrogant; he will cause myriads to perish, but will not prevail.

9. The king of the north will come under the influence of the king of the south; and after that the king of the south will return to his land.

And he will continue some years: i.e. after the death of the king of the north (cp. Genesis 21.21); indicating that he will remain alive. The first king of the south then will die while the king of the north is alive. Then, that king of the north will die during the lifetime of the second king of the south; dying humbled and paying submission to the king of the south.

10-12. We know that the first *king of the south* began mighty, and was afterwards weak. We also know that the king of the north was weak at first; then he prevailed against the king of the south, and afterwards is to be oppressed once more beneath the hand of the king of the south. He is to die in that condition, his first state being weak, and his last state weak. Now, he tells us that after his death his sons will arise and take possession of the kingdom. He does not tell us their number. However, they are governors, each having an army under him, one of them being chief in power with the others beneath him. And they said: 'Let us do as the second king of the south did, and let us take vengeance from him for our father;' and they all agreed to this.

And his sons will war: he does not say for what. I imagine that they sent him messengers demanding that he

179

yield up the cities which he took from their father, or restore some of the tribute which he imposed upon him. To this he did not consent. So, they collected an army and began to occupy city after city of the territories of the king of the south, the king of the south not moving from his place for fear of them.

First he says and **his sons will war**, to signify that they sent messengers to the king of the south; afterwards **and he will come on, and overflow**, referring to the one of them who was most illustrious.

And he will return and contend: i.e. first he took certain cities from the king of the south; but he did not venture to come to the capital of the king of the south. However, when he saw that the king of the south did not move out against him, he did venture, and attacked him in his capital; even to his fortress.

Thereupon the king of the south was compelled to come out against him.

And will fight with him, even with the king of the north: probably he directed his energies first against the armies, then against the king himself. When the latter saw he was attacked, he set up a mighty army before him, to repel the king of the south or, if possible, defeat him. Thereupon the king of the south becomes master of the mighty army gathered by the king of the north, and his heart is lifted up, and the king of the north flees by himself and returns to his city.

And he will cast down tens of thousands: i.e. he took captive as many as he wished of the army of the king of the north, and killed a multitude of the soldiers and of others.

But he will not prevail: i.e. no one will be able to stand before him. All will flee before him. During a long period he will be like this; -- I am inclined to think the KING of the SOUTH who burnt the Temple and carried our people captive is meant; from which time the Romans have been strong, their empire has prevailed, and they have become a 'mighty terrible monster.' You must know that these wars covered many years, about two hundred; the pronouns therefore do not refer to individuals, but to the empire.

¹³Then the king of the north will again muster a multitude even greater than the first. After a time, a matter of years, he will advance with a great army and much baggage. ¹⁴In those times, many will resist the king of the south, and the lawless sons of your people will assert themselves to confirm the vision, but they will fail.

13. Probably this **king of the north** is not the same as the one who fled. He is to gather armies **greater than the former**, which were taken by the king of the south.

And at the end of the times, years (instead of 'at the end of years') refers to the prophecy of the seventy weeks. Or, it may mean after the *end of years* during which there was an agreement between them, made after the defeat, and they obeyed the king of the south because of his power. After the end of this period the king of the north will collect these armies and attack the king of the south, *v. infra*.

14. In ver. 13 he said **at the end of the times, years**: now he goes back and tells us how in those times the power of the king of the south will be great, and he will collect mighty armies, whereas the king of the north will be low.

The children of the breakers of your people refers, it is said, to the followers of Jesus, said by the Christians to be the Messiah; those followers who made the Gospel. Their names are well known:

1. Matthew the publican, 2. Mark the fisherman, 3. Luke the physician, disciple of Paulus Abu-Shaoul, 4. John, kinsman of Jesus, entrusted by him with certain powers.

These are called **children of the breakers of your people** because they made a breach in the religion; and doubtless multitudes of Israelites became Christians with them.

Will lift themselves up: in that they got a great and mighty station, and a mighty name.

To establish: i.e. their purpose was to *establish the vision* in

182

Jesus' favor, as is known from their profession in their gospels and records.

But they will fall: if this refers to the followers of Jesus, it will mean 'they will leave the religion;' if to the nation of Israel, then it means that Israel after this will fall. How many Israelites will have been slain from that time until God will deliver His people! That then will be the meaning of **they will fall** indicating that the ruin of Israel was by and through the Christians. First we were ruined by our kings and false prophets, who were the cause of the cessation of our empire and of our captivity; then these Christians have been the cause of our ruin and destruction during the Captivity; and some went astray at the beginning of the empire of the Little Horn, and also ruined us.

¹⁵The king of the north will advance and throw up siege ramps and capture a fortress city, and the forces of the south will not hold out; even the elite of his army will be powerless to resist. ¹⁶His opponent will do as he pleases, for none will hold out against him; he will install himself in the beautiful land with destruction within his reach.

15. After the digression in which he introduces the history of Jesus and his followers, and what is to come upon us through them, he goes back and finishes what becomes of the king of the north after he has collected the armies. The words **so the king of the north will come** are to be connected with **and he will come** on in ver. 13b. The king of the north is to come to the land of Rome and besiege the capital city and take it (**and take a well-fenced city**); i.e. *Constantinople*.

And the arms of the south: i.e. 'the many who will stand up' (ver. 14), great armies collected by the king of the south to help him.

His chosen people: hosts wherein he placed special confidence. These, too, cannot stand before the king of the north, who slays multitudes of the hosts of the king of the south, while many more desert to him and help him; *v. infra.*

16. **He who comes to him**: the deserters from the king of the south; mighty men of valor, who will do the will of the king of the north, and open gates for him. He will make them governors in the territory of Rome, after which none of the countries of the king of the south will stand before him. At that time the Romans will have spread over the land of Israel, and be in possession of it, especially of the holy city, having great hosts in it; and the king of the north will attack them with his armies, and will remain in the land of Israel a long time, and will slay a multitude of Romans (and will destroy with his hand).

¹⁷He will set his mind upon invading the strongholds throughout his [foe's] kingdom, but in order to destroy it he will effect an agreement with him and give him a daughter in marriage; he will not succeed at it and it will not come about. ¹⁸He will turn to the coastlands and capture many; but a consul will put an end to his insults, nay pay him back for his insults.

17. The king of the north will attack the fortresses of the king of the south with his armed men.

And upright ones with him: (according to some) certain Israelite *Scribes* etc. who will be with him, and inform him of what is written concerning his invasion, whose words he will believe **and do** thereafter.

The daughter of the women: the holy city, it is said; indicating that he is to ravage certain places consecrated to Roman worship, and their royal palace. Maybe God will give him power over the king of the south, and let him do this to him, in return for what the king of the south did to the Second Temple, and with Israel; so that this will be some consolation to His people.

Then he tells us that the king of the north will not stay in Syria, nor will the country remain under his authority. He will turn away then to another place, and the Romans will be established there as before.

18. **He will invade the islands belonging to the king of the south**: referring perhaps to the 'frontier-land,' sc. Tarsus, Cyprus, etc., which he will conquer, slaying and plundering, not intending to remain in the territory of the south, but only to take reprisals for what the king of the south did to him. The king of the south had put to shame the king of the north by what he had done to him when he attacked him *in his fortress*. So, when the king of the north does all this to the king of the south, the *reproach offered* by the latter will be taken away. A captain, sc. the king of the north, **will cause the reproach offered by him to cease**.

185

Moreover, he will cause his reproach to turn upon him: i.e. not only does he cause the reproach offered by him to cease, but in his turn he brings reproach upon the king of the south. The king of the south, who burnt the holy city, had not attacked the king of the north. Only after he had been attacked by the latter did he do as described to the latter's army. This king, on the other hand, invades his capital, kills his soldiers, takes many cities, and massacres their inhabitants; thus doing more than the king of the south had done to him. Therefore, he says moreover, etc.

The above has been an account of the relations between the king of the north and the king of the south, including three events:

(1) and (2) The armies of the king of the south attack the king of the north.

(3) The king of the north attacks the king of the south. The first and second of these campaigns were won by the king of the south against the king of the north. In the third, the reverse took place. The king of the south conquered twice, the king of the north once. These three events took place during a long period, more than three hundred years, as we have explained above. The seat of the king of the north was in the province of Baghdad. This is the last war between the two kings.

¹⁹He will head back to the strongholds of his own land, but will stumble, and fall, and vanish. ²⁰His place will be taken by one who will dispatch an officer to exact tribute for royal glory, but he will be broken in a few days, not by wrath or by war.

19. After doing all this he will return to Baghdad, his royal seat: and afterwards will stumble in the place of his throne. Maybe some of his servants will slay him, and the matter will be concealed (and will not be found).

20. **In his place**: i.e. the second will sit in the place of the first. Had he not stated this, it might have been in another place. In his place, there will sit another without strength, or victory, or war. Two facts are told us about him:

    1. **Cause the tax collector to pass.**
    2. **Glory of the kingdom.**

With regard to the first, some scholars have asserted that he abolished the taxes, and that during his time there was no trouble, vexation or affliction imposed by him on the people. Other scholars assert that he obliged the people to lock their doors at midday, and occupy themselves with eating and drinking - the weak among them having supplies from the royal table; so that the time passed in eating, drinking, amusement, enjoyment, and the wearing of new and fine apparel. Consequently, the words **the glory of the kingdom** are written. He tells us, however, that his time will not be long (within few days). He will die without attack or war. Those who know this history tell us that the Arabs seized the place while the people were engaged in eating and drinking. They seized the king and killed him. He was last of the *Magus* who reigned in Baghdad; from whom the Arab kings, who still hold it, took it.

187

²¹His place will be taken by a contemptible man, on whom royal majesty was not conferred; he will come in unawares and seize the kingdom through trickery. ²²The forces of the flood will be overwhelmed by him and will be broken, and so too the covenant leader. ²³And, from the time an alliance is made with him, he will practice deceit; and he will rise to power with a small band.

21. **A contemptible person**: every king of the dynasties mentioned to this point had possessed some spirit and generosity except this one, who had none. His story is well known, so we need not expand on it.

He will come with security: i.e. he will enter city after city without war or siege, which his predecessors had used.

And will obtain the kingdom by flatteries: i.e. his professed 'visions,' and the rest of what was described in chap. 7, 'the mouth that speaks great things,' etc.; and in chap. 10, 'understanding dark sayings.'

22. **The arms of a flood**: great armies of the king of the north, and the armies of Rome also. They will flee before him and be dispersed.

And with the prince of the covenant: said to be the ruler of Rome, compare 9.26; called *of the covenant* because he had made a covenant with Israel, *ibid.* 27. Others make it refer to the *kings of Israel* beneath whom the sons of David were afflicted.

23. **After the league**: said to refer to a follower of the 'Man of Wind ' (Muhammad), Omar one of the 'ten.' He will deal deceitfully with Israel, and others. Their story is well known. He will come up and become strong with a few helpers.

²⁴He will invade the richest of provinces unawares, and will do what his father and forefathers never did, lavishing on them^a spoil, booty, and wealth; he will have designs upon strongholds, but only for a time. ²⁵"He will muster his strength and courage against the king of the south with a great army. The king of the south will wage war with a very great and powerful army but will not stand fast, for they will devise plans against him. ²⁶Those who eat of his food will ruin him. His army will be overwhelmed, and many will fall slain.

24. **With security** in verse 21 referred to the 'Man of Wind;' here it refers to Omar.

The fattest places of the province: the great cities where the rich live.

He will do, etc.: in the way of conquest and massacre. His predecessors, he says, did not reached such distinction as he.

He will scatter among them prey, etc.: he himself was satisfied with meager food, coarse clothing, and humble belongings. Whenever he took a city and plundered it, he gave all the plunder to the soldiers, and took none for himself.

Prey may refer to men, whom he used to take captive; or to precious objects and instruments.

Spoil: garments.

Substance: beasts of burden, cattle and sheep.

Against the strongholds: certain fortresses in the province of Iraq, that belonged to the king of the north, which he took by plots and strategy.

Even for a time: until the end of *his progress*; when the time of his retrogression comes, his position will be reversed.

25. **He will stir up his power**: this means that the king of the south had made no preparations, while he had with

---

^a *I.e., his followers.*

him only the handful of men who were with him at the beginning of his career (**with a few men**, ver. 23). However, it came to pass that new people became Moslems continually, so his army grew great.

This battle was fought between Omar ibn EI-Khattab and the Romans in Syria. Omar, the historians say, entered Jerusalem, and the king of Rome prepared to fight with him. They battled in the plain of Amwas, near Jerusalem. Omar is said to have had a mighty army, and for this reason the king of the south met him also with a mighty army. The Roman army, though, was greater than the Moslem, as is implied by the additional words in the text.

But he will not stand: sc. the army of the king of the south. Indeed it took to flight as soon as they joined battle.

For they will devise: his army will. When they saw the Moslem general approach they abandoned the king of the south; even the chosen youths who were fed from his table destroyed him: for they were not true to him in the war.

Thereupon the Moslems became masters of the Romans, and killed a vast number of them (**many will fall down slain**); and the Moslems took the land of Israel from the Romans, and hold it to this day.

²⁷The minds of both kings will be bent on evil; while sitting at the table together, they will lie to each other, but to no avail, for there is yet an appointed term.

27. He said above **they set not upon him** (ver. 21); and indeed so long as he had not taken the holy city from the Romans he does not call him their king. Now they have taken it, he calls him so.

Both these kings: i.e. of Arabia and Rome.

Their hearts will be to do mischief: i.e. they will do some harm to Israel, each of them, in some fashion; as it is well known that the Moslems and Christians do.

Against one table: to be referred, it is said, to Israel; called one table because Edom and Ishmael eat each other's food. Compare 11.43 with comm. There he spoke of their mixing in marriage; no less do they mix in the matter of food. Isaiah speaks of both, chap. 46, where *they, that sanctify themselves* are the uncircumcised, who profess *sanctity* and speak of *Saint* So-and-so, and how the time of sanctification is come, and have *offerings*. They profess that they have holy priests, and baptismal water, and consequently do not wash off pollution. As for the Moslems they do not hold that view, but do wash after pollution. Consequently, they are called by the prophet *they that purify themselves*. Accordingly, the uncircumcised use the word *sanctify*, and the others the word *purity*. *To the gardens* refers to the fact that both profess that the 'Garden' (i.e. Paradise) is for them, as is stated in their books and commonly declared by them. *Behind one in the midst* refers to the fact that they all agree that the *Law* is superseded, and that another system has been delivered since, that system being a religion not to be superseded by another. So when Islam started, they said of the Law just what the Christians had said. Furthermore, they asserted that the Book of their founder had superseded the religion of the Christians with another. Then he informs us that the professors of

191

sanctity eat *swine's flesh,* while the professors of purity eat *abominations and the mouse.* For although Islam forbids swine's flesh, still otherwise they do not abstain from eating the food of the uncircumcised, so that they may be said to eat at one table, whereas Israel form one table - since they eat neither swine's flesh nor abominations nor the mouse. From this point of view, therefore, the words **at one table** refer to Israel. If we can make *at one table* signify two things, one will be that they *sit at one table,* the other that they *lie* against God and His people.

It will not prosper: i.e. Israel; their affairs will not prosper, and they will be afflicted and abandoned.

The end remains to the time: i.e. until the end of the four kingdoms comes; when Edom and Ishmael will fail and turn back, and Israel prosper. The verse covers the long period from the rise of Islam to the end of the Captivity.

²⁸He will return to his land with great wealth, his mind set against the holy covenant. Having done his pleasure, he will return to his land. ²⁹At the appointed time, he will again invade the south, but the second time will not be like the first.

28. The speaker returns to complete what preceded. (In the preceding verse the ruin and death which were to fall on the king of the south were mentioned.) He informs us how the ruler of Islam will return to the place where his station was. This is said to have been Damascus, where, therefore he returned, with *great riches* plundered from the army of the king of the south.

And his heart will be to hurt Israel; cp. ver. 27 a. The person alluded to is known to have been a bitter enemy of Israel (Omar ibn EI-Khattab).

And he will do his pleasure in Israel by decrees which he proclaimed against them. These are the Jews established in the holy city. After this he will return to his own city.

This was the battle which ended unfavorably for the king of Rome at the holy city.

29. With this verse ends the account of what happened at the rise of the power of Ishmael. From this verse commences the notice of what is to happen at the close of their power. In the previous verse he said **the end remains to the time,** indicating that when the time appointed came and he arrived at the end of his career, he would **return, and come into the south,** i.e. enter into the Roman territory. This began some years ago in the west, when the king of the west; who is now the king of Egypt, sent armies into the Roman territory.

But it will not be as the former refers to what happened at the rise of his dynasty: (1) his overthrowing three thrones (chap. 7.5); (2) Ezra 25.

Or as the latter refers to what will be explained on ver. 40. The first battles were all advantageous to Ishmael and against the king of the south. The last will all be advantageous to the king of the south and against Ishmael. This intermediate battle will be unlike either, and from an intermediate king.

³⁰Ships from Kittim will come against him. He will be checked, and will turn back, raging against the holy covenant. Having done his pleasure, he will then attend to those who forsake the holy covenant. ³¹Forces will be levied by him; they will desecrate the temple, the fortress; they will abolish the regular offering and set up the appalling abomination.

30. **There will enter into it inhabitants of the desert and Cyprians** refers perhaps to their entering into his religion; or possibly under his rule.

And will be broken: to be construed, not with *him*, but with the *people and countries;* every one of them will be overthrown before him.

And will have indignation against the holy covenant: the king referred to began by attacking Israel with injuries; then he left them. At the end, he will return to them. This is an event in the future. It bas not yet come to pass.

He will even return and have regard to them that forsake refers to certain Israelites who abandoned the religion of Israel and entered into his religion, to whom he will show favor. Evidently he will require them to abandon their religion: some will remain true to the religion of Israel, against whom he will be indignant. Others will abandon it, and enter his religion, to whom he will show favor. We will explain this at the end of the chapter.

31. He tells us first that he will fight with the king of the south (ver. 29); then the condition of Israel during his time. Then he goes back to tell us what he will do with his people.

Arms: certain hosts that will penetrate into their holy place, and do the following things:

(1). **They will profane the sanctuary, even the fortress:** i.e. the place mentioned in chap. 8.11.

The term there used was 'cast down;' here, **profane**. The first indicates that he will destroy it, and raze it to the ground; the second, that their dead bodies will be thrown into it, so that it will become like a dung-pit or dirt-heap.

(2). **They will remove the continual**: i.e. they will put a stop to the Hagg (pilgrimage); men will not go on pilgrimages there after this, or pray, or celebrate the tenth day according to their custom. It is called *continual* because the institution was perpetual. They never relaxed the Hagg. Compare 8.11, except that here is added--

(3). **And they will set up the abomination that makes desolate**: most probably referring to the images in that house (cp. 2 Kings 11.8, and Deuteronomy 29.17). These images were very ancient. He had not been able to remove them originally, so he removed them now. Reference is made to the same subject in Psalms 53.20. Observe that in the 'Vision' he mentioned several things collectively, which here he separates. If the words **they will set up the abomination that makes desolate** refer to the image itself, it must mean that it will be left fallen, after having been erect and protected. However, if we refer them to its *face*, then the meaning will be that *face* will be left *desolate*, waste, un-approached. This is alluded to by the prophet Isaiah in his prayer (10-15.2), where the *place* is the house, said to belong to *strangers* because these images are in it, *never to be built for ever* because it is waste, and never to be rebuilt. If, thirdly, we refer it to its worshippers, it will mean that they will grieve at the ruin that has overtaken their sanctuary, even as Israel has grieved ever since ruin overtook *them*, and *their* sanctuary was laid waste.

196

³²He will flatter with smooth words those who act wickedly toward the covenant, but the people devoted to their God will stand firm. ³³The knowledgeable among the people will make the many understand; and for a while they shall fall by sword and flame, suffer captivity and spoliation.

32. A further explanation of the words **he will have regard to them that forsake**, etc.

He will deceive them by soft, flattering words; i.e. some will go out from our people for certain worldly reasons, and will take verses of the Scripture about the Messiah that they will apply to the temporal ruler, explaining away the words *Sabbath and feast*, ruining themselves and departing from religion. They are said to **do wickedly against the covenant** because they do wrong, and shake off the yoke of the law and the covenants of Israel.

But the people that know his God will be strong refers to certain Israelites who will understand the system of the temporal LORD. They will know that he has a secret many Israelites did not understand, and so perished. But some--scholars--will investigate his religion, see that it is false, cling to the law, act according to it, and not depart from the religion of Israel as others did. The fulfillment of this began in the West many years ago, when many Israelites gave up their religion and adopted his; as is well known. Those who do not give up the faith are called **the people that know his God**.

33. The **wise** are the same as the last.

Will instruct many: i.e. they will cause many Israelites to understand his system, strengthen their hands in the religion of God, and will not abandon the faith. Now, when he sees that they do not enter into his religion, his wrath will become fierce against them, as was Nebuchadnezzar's against Hananiah, Mishael, and Azariah, so that he threw them into a fiery furnace. So will this prince deal with Israel. Some he

197

will kill with the *sword*, others by *fire*. Some he will afflict by *captivity* or by *plundering* their slaves and property.

Days: the period of a year, perhaps. Note the order: (1) **He will have indignation;** (2) **Arms will stand.** (3) **Such as do wickedly against the covenant.**

This shows that a *tribulation* will come upon Israel before the destruction of the house: which the present verse explains.

They will fall: the people who follow the *wise*. The *wise* being spoken of in the following verse.

[34]In defeat, they will receive a little help, and many will join them insincerely. [35]Some of the knowledgeable will fall, that they may be refined and purged and whitened until the time of the end, for an interval still remains until the appointed time.

34. After saying that they will **fall**, he tells us that **when they will fall they will be helped**; not specifying how. Some have thought that God Almighty will raise up for them a savior like Esther the Queen. Others suppose they will be helped by God's destroying the official commissioned with their hurt.

But many will join themselves to them refers perhaps to the deserters. This particular word being used of those who enter a religion; cp. Isaiah 56.6. In spite then of God's helping those who fall 'by the sword and the flame,' many will adopt this man's religion, owing to the flattery he will employ with them. With these **flatteries** compare *supra 21*. This prince then, too, has *flatteries* he uses to draw men into his faith.

35. He tells us first what will happen to the followers of the teachers, how they will fall, but how God will help them and deal mercifully with them; then what he will do with the wise themselves. They too, he says, will fall.

The terms **to refine and to purify** etc. are used of **the teachers**, but not of their followers, because the followers *merely follow* their predecessors, and when they see the teachers fall, their hands will be weakened. If the *falling* of the teachers comes by sword and flame, they will say 'if God has delivered over our teachers, what can we expect?' Their hands will therefore be weakened, for they will say 'if our religion were true, God would not have delivered up our teachers, even as He did not deliver up Hananiah, Mishael, and Azariah.' If however *they will fall* refers to their *leaving the faith* like *supra* 14, of the disciples of Jesus, this will be worse than their death. They will say 'had our religion been true, our teachers would not have departed from it, but would have remained in it, even as Hananiah, Mishael, and Azariah did.' **Therein will he the test**: since he that will withstand will not be affected by what happens to the teachers. He whose faith is not good, though, will depart from the religion. Therefore, he says to refine and purify, which we will explain on 12.10. Then he states that this will happen to them and to the teachers when some time still remains before the end.

³⁶"The king will do as he pleases; he will exalt and magnify himself above every god, and he will speak awful things against the God of gods. He will prosper until wrath is spent, and what has been decreed is accomplished. ³⁷He will not have regard for the god of his ancestors or for the one dear to women; he will not have regard for any god, but will magnify himself above all. ³⁸He will honor the god of fortresses on his stand; he will honor with gold and silver, with precious stones and costly things, a god that his ancestors never knew. ³⁹He will deal with fortified strongholds with the help of an alien god. He will heap honor on those who acknowledge him, and will make them master over many; he will distribute land for a price.

36-39. **Will do according to his will**: possibly he refers to the empire generally, from the establishment of the state of Ishmael to the end of their history, in his account of the ten things beginning with **will do** and ending with **divide for a price**. Or he may refer to the most important of these terms, who will waste the sanctuary, and stop the Hagg. Both views are possible. Now we have already heard what he will do with Edom, Israel, and the sanctuary. So, he now goes back to tell us the general principles of his conduct.

(1) **He will do according to his will**: compare what we said about the 'ram' and the 'he-goat.' It means that his commands are carried out, that he does what he pleases, that no one opposes his will, or contends against him, owing to the might of his state; and that he attains what he desires.

(2) **And he will exalt himself and magnify himself above every god**: observe that in this chapter six *gods* are mentioned:

a. **he will magnify himself above every god.**
b. **Will speak marvelous things against the GOD of gods.**
c. **Neither will he regard the gods of his fathers.**
d. **Nor regard any god.**
e. **he will honor the god of fortresses.**

201

f. god whom his fathers knew not.

None of these except b refers to the Creator (cp. Deuteronomy 10.17). The rest refer to deities other than Him. It is said of three of these that he will not respect them, but magnify himself against them. Two of them, though, will be honored by him (e and f). We are not told whether he will or will not serve the Creator, but merely that *he will speak marvelous things,* cp. 7.25. Why does he say of the *god of fortresses* that he will *honor* him, not *serve* him, and of all besides the Creator and *e* and *f* that he will not *regard* them? Most probably it means that he will profess to serve the Almighty Creator, but will say what is impossible of him. If it refers to the *kingdom* (i.e. the Caliphate) since its rise, the fact is shown in their language and the popular belief. However, if it refers to *this last,* then it is again a statement about the system which he will spread. Of the other deities he says **he will magnify himself above all**; which does not mean that he will *magnify himself* against the idols themselves, but against their worshippers; for he will revile their creeds.

Neither will he regard the god of his fathers refers to the creeds of his fathers who served idols, if Pasul (Muhammad) is meant; if *the last* is indicated, it will mean that he will annul their present system, and in consequence ravage the house.

Nor the desire of women: Jerusalem, which the peoples and nations used to glorify. He arranged that it should no longer be the Qiblalh turning his back to it, and his face to the place where they went on pilgrimage. If it refers to *the last king,* it will refer to the house where the pilgrims went, which he will destroy. Very likely, however, the words *the desire of women* refer to a male image kept in their Qiblah; hence the words come between *the god of his fathers* and *any god,* indicating that it refers to a *special* idol.

Regard signifies *turn to*; observe this, because the word occurs three times in this passage (once in ver. 30, twice in this verse), and the meaning in all three is the same.

The god of fortresses: either the name of a particular idol. Alat or El-Uzza as some have thought--both are familiar--or some other. The word *Mauzzim* may refer to a particular people of that name, mentioned again in ver. 39. They then will have a god and a religion that he will think fit to respect and not overthrow. This god he will **honor** merely; the other he will **honor with gold and silver**, etc.

And with pleasant things: i.e. handsome vessels (Ezra 8.17).

And he will deal with etc. may mean one of two things: (1) he will war with them because they will not obey him. Those that submit to him and adopt his creed will receive honor from him, and gifts and promotion (who ever acknowledges him, etc.). (2) the last clause explains how *He will deal with them*, viz. who ever acknowledges, he will honor. Apparently, then, these *Mauzzim* have two creeds or two idols; one of which he will uphold (ver. 38 a), but not the other (with a strange god). There will be a variety then in their creeds; and this king will approve of one idol to be worshipped, but not the other. We are told of three things that he will do with those who agree to his tenets:

a. **He will increase their glory**: referring to the wealth and office that he will bring them.

b. **He will cause them to rule over many**.

c. He will give them lands; **he will divide land for a price**, i.e. lands of high value. It may mean that he will make this serve for a price, the price for discarding their faith and adopting his. And it is this which will ruin those 'that forsake the holy covenant.' When they see that all who adopt his faith are elevated to these stations, whereas those who will not assent to his tenets are killed or burnt. They will therefore abandon their religion. Through this, great multitudes of our

203

people have been ruined, from the foundation of this empire until now. Many, too, in the West have apostatized. As for Israel, when God showed His wonders in Egypt and Sinai, the people ('the mixed multitude') believed in *their* religion for fear of the sword, not in hope of promotion. What God has enjoined on us in our Law is that if any one becomes a proselyte, we are to feed him with our food as we feed the orphans or widows (Deuteronomy 24.19), but by no means to confer upon him eminent rank [because of his conversion].

And he will prosper (ver. 36) shows that he will succeed in all his doings, until the wrath of God against his people has ended. After the reign of this dynasty, there will be no other. It is the last of the dynasties that will oppress Israel.

⁴⁰At the time of the end, the king of the south will lock horns with him, but the king of the north will attack him with chariots and riders and many ships. He will invade lands, sweeping through them like a flood; ⁴¹he will invade the beautiful land, too, and many will fall, but these will escape his clutches: Edom, Moab, and the chief part of the Ammonites. ⁴²He will lay his hands on lands; not even the land of Egypt will escape. ⁴³He will gain control over treasures of gold and silver and over all the precious things of Egypt, and the Libyans and Cushites will follow at his heel.

40. **And at the time of the end**: this expression includes two things: (1) the *end* of the success of this dynasty; (2) the *end* of the indignation against Israel.

In the end, then, the tables will be turned. At the first *appearance* of the 'Little Horn,' it warred with the king of the south and took from him three thrones, as we explained at 7.24, viz. Syria and the capitals. Then, it took Iraq and Khorasan from him. It went on conquering and taking *city* after *city* (*cp.* ver. 24) up to the Caspian Gates. However, when his success comes to an end, these two kings--of the north and of the south--will turn against him (here a and b). Some portion of the operations of the king of the south has been realized in our time. I refer to certain battles where he has taken from the Moslems *Antioch*, *Tarsus*, *Ayin Zarba*, and that region. More events, though, are still to come. The king of the north, however, has not as yet done anything. He says of the king of the south that he will *push at him*, because he is near him, and will come from near Syria. He says of the king of the north that he will *whirl against him*, because he will come from near the Caspian Gates.

We promised that when we came to this verse we would explain the importance of the phrases 'king of the north,' 'king of the south.' Many scholars suppose the king of the north refers to the *king of Arabia*, because the latter took Baghdad from the king of the north, which had been the royal city of the Magus. We will show how this difficulty can be solved.

You must know that the four kingdoms mentioned in the dreams of Nebuchadnezzar and Daniel are divided as follows. The first is a *world-empire*. Now, the rulers of the whole world are not named after any particular quarter, but after their principal city, e.g. king of Babylon; not 'king of the east, west,' etc. No such phrase can be found used of the king of the Chaldees, nor of the kings of the Medes and Persians, nor of Alexander, the first king of the Greeks. Only after his death, when his kingdom was divided among his four scholars (11.4), does he begin to speak of a 'king of the north' or 'of the south.' Now, if the empire of Islam were in any one of the quarters--north or south--he might *very* well use the terms 'king of the north' or 'of the south.' As, however, that empire has seized countries in all four quarters, it cannot be named after any one of them. This principle is obviously correct. The king of Islam then can be neither. Therefore, he says the king of the south will *push at him*, sc. at the king mentioned in ver. 36. If the king of the south *pushes at him*, he cannot be the king of the south. Similarly, he says with reference to him that *the king of the north will whirl against him*, i.e. come against him like a whirlwind. It is clear, then, that the king of Islam cannot be king of the north.

With chariots and with horsemen and with many ships: he does not specify which of the two will come with them. Probably, the king of the north will come to him *with chariots and horsemen*, while the king of the south does so on the sea *with ships*: cp. Num. 24.24.

Observe he *will came*, not *they*; which would have referred to both kings together, so we would have supposed the two would assist each other against him. Now, we would not know which *will come* from the words of Daniel. However, this has been explained by another prophet, Joel son of

206

Bethuel. He has written three chapters (beginning respectively at 1.21, 11.1, and 3.9); the first of which refers to Nebuchadnezzar, the second to the king of the north mentioned here (11.20 *I will remove far off from you the northern;* we will presently explain how this will be) 'the third to Gog.'

The Islamic prince established at Baghdad--not the Abbaside--is from the north. Now, they were originally unbelievers, but will be associated with the Abbaside Caliph. The chief of these *arms* will certainly take that city, sc. Baghdad. They will be beaten back before him; and, perhaps, he will kill some of them. After this, they will rise up against those who repulsed them, and make for Babylon, as the prophets foretold. See Isaiah 13.1, Jeremiah 11. They say of them *they will not refine silver or gold,* inasmuch as they will only desire vengeance for their sufferings at the hands of those who took their city, and will gather together and fight against them. They are referred to here in the words *and the king of the north will sweep against him.* The words *he will enter into the countries, and will overflow and pass through* indicate that he will enter the realm of the king who took Baghdad from the hands of the Abbasides, and will conquer the land of Babylon. At his arrival, a number of Israelites will go out, directing their steps to the land of Israel; cp. Jeremiah 1.5. Then the king of the north will direct his steps towards the territory of this king. He will go out from Babylon to Syria, conquering every city he passes, it not being his primary intention to have a royal throne established for him, but only to destroy the cities that are under the power of the LORD of Islam. He will kill all whom he meets (**he will stretch forth his hand also upon the countries**); and he is to come to the land of Israel (**he will enter also into the glorious land**).

Will be overthrown: i.e. most of the cities and villages in the land of Israel, and all the seacoast.

But these will be delivered out of his hand: Edom, i.e.

Djebel-eshshara, **Moab**, and a portion of the children of **Ammon**. We are not told the reason of this. He cannot pass them over through weakness, since these countries are not more powerful than Babylon and Egypt. Rather, he does not trouble himself about them, seeing that they have no state, royalty or wealth. Therefore, he will not take them into account. Many Israelites, however, will pass over there (cp. Isaiah 16.4). Some have thought they will pass over there before this king. The Scripture moreover (Joel) shows that Israel will be in Zion at the time. Next he will pass over into the **land of Egypt**, that too being Islamitie territory. This is the only country said to be plundered, owing to the treasures and riches it contains (ver. 43).

The Libyans and Ethiopians will be at his steps: certain Ethiopians and Libyans will *follow* him at the time; or, perhaps, on his stay in Egypt he will *destroy* the Ethiopians and Libyans, who are in Egyptian territory.

⁴⁴But reports from east and north will alarm him, and he will march forth in a great fury to destroy and annihilate many. ⁴⁵He will pitch his royal pavilion between the sea and the beautiful holy mountain, and he will meet his doom with no one to help him.

44. **But news will trouble him**: when he comes to the western frontier of the province of Egypt, he will receive *tidings* from the east and the north, sc. of the entrance of Israel from the wilderness into Palestine, as we will explain at length afterwards. When they enter it from the wilderness, they will conquer it, and their enemies will be beaten back before them. When this reaches the king of the north, who will be at the time at the edge of Egypt, he will return to Syria to **destroy and utterly make away with many**, i.e. Israel, who entered in large numbers. But when the news of his return reaches Israel, they will gather together on Mount Zion, and do what Joel says (chap. 11 and fell.). This they will do at the time when he **plants the tents of his palace**. It is thought that he will pitch his tents at Amwas (now, between that place and Jerusalem are four parasangs); or else he will encamp in the wilderness of Tekoa, which also is a vast plain. When he spreads out his tents there, intending to come to them the next morning in Jerusalem, God will send His angel Michael, who will destroy his entire army. They will all die, and remain cast about, rotting on the face of the plain until they decompose and stink (v. Joel 1.50.). Therefore, we know that this section deals with the king of the north, and relates what will happen to Israel at his coming.

"At that time, the great prince, Michael, who stands beside the sons of your people, will appear. It will be a time of trouble, the like of which has never been since the nation came into being. At that time, your people will be rescued, all who are found inscribed in the book.

XII.

1. **And at that time** refers to 11.40; and signifies the times specified in 7.25. **Will stand** (instead of 'will come' or some similar word) shows that the *standing* will last three and a half years. He *will stand* for two purposes: (1) to put an end to the monarchies (v. 10.21); (2) to deliver Israel from certain calamities that are to befall them. Before Michael was called 'your prince;' here the **great prince**, showing that he is a mighty angel.

And there will be a time of trouble, such as never was since shows that there can have been nothing *like it* since the confusion of tongues. This is not that there has been nothing of the same *kind*, since there has always been famine, sword, plague, sickness, poverty, and the other things found in the world, nor religious persecution either (we have seen Nebuchadnezzar require Hananiah etc. to worship the image he had made). It can only refer to a state like that which Oded the prophet described to king Asa, when 'there was no peace to him who went out,' etc. (2 Chronicles 15.8; cp. Zechariah 8.10). The chief source of these afflictions is that the 'Arms' will seek to take the kingdom of the Abbasides, coming from Babylon, as the learned tell us. Also, they will prevent the pilgrims from praying in Mecca, where they used to pray, and will destroy the remembrance of the Man of Wind. Then, the sword will come between them, and the 'Arms' will prevail against them, and make mighty havoc among them. Some of them will flee into the 'forest in

Arabia' (Isaiah 21.13), hungry and thirsty; 'for they fled away from the swords.'

The reason for their turning into that region is that they know it is impossible for them to return to their own cities because the *Conspirator* has already taken possession of them. They will take counsel to flee to their kinsmen, who believe as they do, and stay with them. Their kinsmen will come to meet them with food and water to save them. From that time civil war will begin in Ishmael. The *Conspirators*, however, will not get the empire, because their chief will require men to abandon their religion, a religion about four hundred years old, this without any miracle, except the sword. The sword, therefore, will fall among them. At that time the sultan's courts will cease, there will be no longer a royal throne, or business on the roads, or police and guardians in the cities. No shops will open, no merchants travel, no rain will fall from the sky, no husbandman or vine-dresser will exist, no man with any possible means of subsistence. Then the great famine will come, and the great plague, with the sword. Then, the destruction will be accomplished. Only a few men will be left; the cities will be wasted and the roads desolate, the nation occupied with each other. Then Israel will flee out from among them to the 'wilderness of the nations.' The words of the text allude to this condition. The king of the north will come to Babylon, and the Israelites will come out from Babylon into their own land before the great confusion. At that time there will be a disturbance in the land of Israel (?) before they depart (cp. Jeremiah 11.55).

Your people will be delivered: since the destruction will alight upon the Gentiles, as was said before; but from the addition **every one that will be found written in the book** we see that not every Jew will escape, but those that are written, and those only; not the wicked among Israel who did not 'repent at that time' (2 Chronicles 11.16 and

211

Deuteronomy 4.30). Those who repent will survive; but those who do not repent will die by the sword by the hand of the enemy, or by the plague of God (Amos 9.10).

Observe that Isaiah 65 uses the same phrase *(written)* of the works of the wicked that Malachi, in 3.16, uses of those of the righteous. Plainly, the phrase here cannot refer to both good and bad, but must be interpreted as above. This is explained by Isaiah 4.3, 'Every one that is written to life in Jerusalem;' showing that only those will escape who are *written to life* adding afterwards, *when God will have washed away* the filth of the daughters of Zion, indicating that the people *written to life* are those that are washed clean of filth and blood. [Of the others], those that are among the Gentiles will fall by the sword. Those that do not die by their hand, but go out with the people to the 'wilderness of the peoples,' will be killed by God Almighty (Ezekiel 20.38). I cannot possibly give a full account of what will happen at that time, since that would require a book for itself. I have suggested in every book of the three portions of Scripture that I have explained as much as each passage allowed.

²Many of those that sleep in the dust of the earth will awake, some to eternal life, others to reproaches, to everlasting abhorrence.

2. At that time many of the dead will rise. **Many**, as in Ester 8.17; not *all* the dead will rise, but only *some*. We have explained this on Ezekiel 37, at length, and have said a little about it on Job 14.12. Here, let us add a little more. Let us observe, first, that he promises the **deliverance of the nation** (ver. 10); and then the resurrection of the dead; indicating that the living and the dead both will see the salvation. Now, just as he divided the *living* into two portions, one to survive and one to die; so he divides those that are to rise from the dead into two portions, one to everlasting life, and the other to **contempt**. Ezekiel has shown that those who are to rise are people of the Captivity (37.11), 'Behold, they say, our bones are dried up, and our hope is lost,' which is not the condition of those who died under the monarchy. Similarly, Isaiah says (26.19), 'Your dead will live, awake and sing, that dwell in the dust,' which is to be compared with the phrase here, **those who sleep in dust of the ground**; only there the prophet confined himself to the mention of the saints of the nation, where here he speaks of both classes together.

Shame and everlasting contempt: see Isaiah *ad fin:* 'They will look on the carcasses of the men who sinned against the LORD.' This is a description of those who died during the Captivity, having offended God by capital transgressions.

To shame and eternal contempt: shame, because they used to cast reproaches on the best of the nation, who sighed, and were troubled and angry at what had happened to the nation and the house of God (cp. Psalms 69. throughout). They would eat and drink and let their time pass in amusement and enjoyment, which God has forbidden us

213

(Hosea 9.2). It was not sufficient for them ignore what God commanded, but they abhorred those who obeyed Him, and criticised them for practicing the Law, mourning and fasting. Therefore, at the end of the Psalm quoted (ver. 22), he curses them ('Let their table before them become a snare,' etc.). Now, when the Mount of Olives splits, and a vast gorge is formed between the halves, this gorge will become the place of punishment of these wicked ones. Whenever there is a Sabbath-day or a new moon, Israel will go out on the first day of the week or on the second day of the month to these prisoners, and see what has happened to them; cp. Isaiah 65.15. These evildoers used to reprimand the saints wrongfully. They will *reproach* the evildoers justly.

Contempt: when they hear their bitter cry, because of the pain of the fire and the bite of the serpents, for *their worm will never die*; and **eternal**, because there is no end to it. Wherever the word *eternal* occurs there is no proof, intellectual or traditional, that there is an end. On the contrary, reason necessitates that the punishment of the wicked will be everlasting, without term. We must now observe that whenever the text has an intelligible expression with a possible literal meaning, it is not allowable to explain it away by abandoning that literal sense. It is necessary, therefore, that the words **those who sleep in the dust of the earth** must be taken literally, and must not be referred to the people of the Captivity, who, during that captivity, might be compared to the dead; especially as there is nothing in this chapter except what is to be taken literally. We are familiar with the fact that when Daniel saw the vision, Gabriel interpreted it to him because it had an allegorical meaning. However, when he came to the words 'two thousand three hundred,' etc., he said 'the vision is true,' meaning what we have stated there. Similarly, at the beginning of this section, he said, 'I will tell you the truth.' Consequently, this whole

214

section is to be taken literally. Therefore, this verse must be taken literally. Furthermore, this is not refuted either by reason or tradition, as we have shown. Regardless, it has been written in our records that God raised the child of the Shunammite to life, and also the dead man who touched the bones of Elisha. Therefore, since such a thing has happened and is thereby not impossible, the resurrection of the dead of Israel, which God has promised, will be accomplished too. And since he says these **to shame and eternal contempt**, the state of the rewarded and of the punished alike will be everlasting. God will raise the dead of the Captivity at the time of the Deliverance. The dead of the monarchy, on the other hand, will be raised when all the dead rise, to be rewarded or punished, which will be at the *creation of the new heavens and the new earth*. Doubtless some great change will take place in this heaven and earth (see Isaiah 40.26). Job refers to the same (14.12): 'Until there is no more heaven they will not wake.' It is well known among all mankind that the resurrection of the dead will take place when this takes place in the heaven and the earth (Job 50 c.). The resurrection of the dead of Israel, however, will take place before that. This is a mere fragment that we have explained here.

³And the knowledgeable will be radiant like the bright expanse of sky, and those who lead the many to righteousness will be like the stars forever and ever.

3. He divides the living and the dead each into two groups, as we saw above. After that he says **the wise**, separating them from the multitude, to show that their rank is higher than that of the rest of the nation. This all refers to those who will rise from the grave. The brightness of their faces, he says, will be like the color of the firmament-- marvelously bright, like the face of Moses. It is a light with which God will cover them, to show their nobility, while at the same time they take pleasure in it.

Those who turn the many to righteousness: those that turned mankind from error to religion.

The many: so of the priests (Mal. 11.6), 'And turned away *many* from iniquity.' They directed men to religion by teaching them the Commandments of YHWH. At the same time, they turned them from transgression by busying themselves with the Law of YHWH, and praying God to direct them to the knowledge of His statutes. They are *those whose way is perfect*: their prayer is recorded and their words expressed in the twenty-two eight-lined stanzas. They are those who say to him that seeks instruction, *Every one who thirsts, come to the waters*. In Isaiah 52, we are told that *by his knowledge will my righteous servant justify many*: in that chapter the groaning of the *wise*, his griefs, and his great knowledge and piety are recorded. These then are referred to in the words **Those who are wise will shine as the brightness of the firmament**, etc.

Like the stars conveys two ideas: (1) light; (2) perpetuity and eternity. It will not be cut off forever. This God will do with them after he has shown them the *salvation of Israel*, and the rebuilding of Jerusalem. They will live a while until they have seen this, and then God will send them to the place of

216

reward. Maybe they will be with the angels above (cp. Zecharia 3.7), in return for their teaching Israel the Law, turning them from their sins, lamenting during the Captivity, and forcing themselves to grieve. Others engaged Israel in the study of traditions, took their goods, fattened their bodies with food and drink, and died merry, not doing their duty, but causing men to sin. They taught them what would make God angry with them. Unquestionably, therefore, their punishment will be far more severe than that of their followers.

⁴"But you, Daniel, keep the words secret, and seal the book until the time of the end. Many will range far and wide and knowledge will increase."

4. Up to this point, the angel has been explaining what is to happen from the time at which he is speaking until the end of the world, as he said, 'I have come to tell you what will be until the end...'

And you Daniel close these words: i.e. leave them as they are. Do not ask for more to be revealed than has been told you.

And seal the book: 'seal this book of yours at what has been told you, and expect no more.' Nothing else could be revealed to him about the matter. Therefore he said this, showing him that there was nothing left to be told him.

To the time of the end: showing that it would not be revealed to any one until the end of the Captivity. Any one who professes to know the end of the Captivity is a deceiver.

Many will run back and forth: i.e. the wise and the seekers of knowledge. This *running back and forth* may be of two kinds: (1) They will run over the countries in search of knowledge, because scholars will be found in every region. The seekers of knowledge, therefore, will go back and forth to learn from them; this is expressed by Amos (8.12). This will be at the beginning of their career; when they seek so passionately, God will make revelations to them. (2) They will *run back and forth* in God's Torah like those who seek treasures, and thereafter, **knowledge will increase**; knowledge of two things: (a) the *commandments*; (b) the *end*. God will not reveal the end until they know the commandments. They are the men that fear the LORD, who are *in possession of his secrets*, which cannot be obtain except by study, search and inquiry into the Torah of God: compare the prayers *teach me o LORD, the way of Your statutes, open my eyes*. These and similar expressions show the vanity of the profession of the *traditionalists* like *El-Fayyumi*, who have destroyed Israel by their writings. They who maintain that the Commandments of God cannot be known by study, because it leads to contradictions; so that we must follow the tradition of the successors of the prophets, viz. the authors of the Mishnah and Talmud, all whose sayings are from God. He has led men astray by his lying books, and vouches for the veracity of any one who lies against God. He will be punished therefore more severely than they, and God will take vengeance for his people from him and those who are like him.

⁵Then I, Daniel, looked and saw two others standing, one on one bank of the river, the other on the other bank of the river. ⁶One said to the man clothed in linen, who was above the water of the river, "How long until the end of these awful things?"

5. After Daniel had heard all that was said to him, from the angel who was addressing him alone (no other angels being present). When the angel had finished his speech, he saw two other angels, one with him in the region where he was standing accompanied by the other on the other side.

Other two: this may indicate one of three things: (1) That he knew that they were not the same angels whom he had seen in the 'Vision' (8.13), when one asked the other about what Daniel was thinking, and the other answered him; as one of the angels here, too, asks the other *how long* etc., we might have thought they were the same. The word other is therefore inserted to show that this is not so.

(2) The word *other* may be intended to show us that the author does not refer to the two angels already mentioned in this chapter (11.16, 18), but to two others; in which case he will at this time have seen *five* angels; two mentioned above and three here.

(3) The word *other* may be intended to prevent our thinking that they were the great angel and another; by its insertion we know that there were *three* angels.

6. **And he said to the man**: i.e. one of the angels (not the plural, in which case we might have thought that both had asked him). *Which* of the two we do not know; nor does he tell him why he saw the one who neither asked or answered. Most likely the one who asked was standing on the other side; while the one who stood with him was intended to relieve his fears, or to bring Daniel to hear the question and the answer. Up to this point, we did not know that the great angel was standing. Here, he explains that he was standing in the air above the water. He was not one of the angels who routinely

220

descend from heaven, having been sent by God for Daniel's sake only.

How long will it be to the end of these wonders? The **wonders** are these *tribulations*, which will come to pass at the last time. **How long?** what will be their duration?

He answered just as Palmoni answered the first questioner (8.13). It was not the questioner's object to *find out himself*. The angels know the mystery that is *closed up*. He only asks so Daniel may hear the answer. If any one asks why the angel did not tell Daniel what he had planned without a question, we answer: perhaps the angel *wouldn't* have given it without question, as the matter is one of the great mysteries.

⁷Then I heard the man dressed in linen, who was above the water of the river, swear by the Ever-Living One as he lifted his right hand and his left hand to heaven: "For a ^atime, times, and half a time;^{-a} and when the breaking of the power of the holy people comes to an end, then shall all these things be fulfilled."

⁸I heard and did not understand, so I said, "My lord, what will be the outcome of these things?"

7. Notice, too, that he does not answer without an *oath*. The angel, he says, **swore an oath**, to show that there can be no alteration; for it is a period of great length. This oath was not for *Daniel's* sake, but for Israel's, the Israel that will be in the time of tribulation. Two things mark the force of this oath: (1) He raised both hands. Now, an oath with both hands raised is the most forcible kind; cp. Genesis 14.2, and 'I have raised my hand,' said by the Creator in a number of places. (2) He swears by the name of God; the most powerful oath, there is none more powerful (cp. Jeremiah 24.26).

By him who lives forever: the Blessed Creator lives eternally. The Hebrew word yH means (1) *living*, e.g. Genesis 6.19; (2) as a substantive, *life*, e. g. by the life of Pharaoh, *ibid.* 42.16. Here it must be interpreted as (1).

He swore **that it will be for a time, times, and a half**; exactly the same as the period mentioned in 7.25.

Here we will collect the passages wherein the *times* connected with the *end* are mentioned. They are eight in all.

(1) Isaiah 16.14. *Within three years, as the years of a hireling, and the glory of Moav will be brought into contempt.*

(2) Isaiah 10-11.16. *Within a year, according to the years of a hireling, and all the glory of Kedar will fall*

(3) Dan. 7.25. *And they will be given into his hand until a time, and times, and a half time.*

(4) Dan. 8.14. *To two thousand and three hundred evenings and*

---

mornings.

(5) Dan. 11.33. *They will fall by the sword and by flame, by captivity and by spoil, many days.*

(6) The present passage.

(7) *infra* 11.

(8) *infra* 12.

Of (1) (three years) we know both the beginning and the end. It begins when 'Moab comes to his sanctuary to pray, and is not able' (ver. 11), i.e. *when the pilgrims desire to pray, but are prevented by the Arms,* as we have explained above. It *ends* when 'the glory of Moab is brought into contempt' (ver. 14), i.e. when they become feeble and few in number, small and of no account *(ibid.),* with no *ruler* at their head *(ibid.).*

(2) Commences when 'those that would pray' flee into the forest in Arabia (Isaiah 21.13; v. *supra*) and ends when 'all the glory of Kedar will fall;' when no 'glory' will be left to Kedar, and their mighty men will be few. This is one of the above three years. When one of those years has passed their glory will fall. At the end of the *three* it will be brought into contempt; i.e. no glory will be left them at all.

(3) Means, as we have said, either that the time he will take for his work in Ishmael and Israel is a 'time, times, and. half a time;' or that Israel will be in the hands of this Conspirator until that period is left until the end. Most probably, in my opinion, this person, who is said to be about to put a stop to the pilgrimage, to destroy the house, and to overthrow the religion of Israel, will continue to do so until that period commences. At that time, he will die, 'be broken without hand;' so that it does not refer to the duration of his power. Rather, when his reign is over, that period will commence. When that period commences, the *tribulations* will commence *(v. supra).* When it ends, they will end. This may be seen from the expression here, **it will be for a time, times, and a half; and when they have made an end of**

223

breaking in pieces the power of the holy people, all these things will be finished. It is clear, therefore, that the tribulations will begin when the times begin, and end when they end.

(4) The *two thousand and three hundred* have already been shown to be 11350 days. The author says they end when *holiness will be justified*. Their beginning is not told us. Most probably the *tribulations* will remain upon Israel from the time of the king who will destroy Mecca and throw the religion of Israel down to the ground for *two thousand three hundred mornings and evenings*. For one year out of this they will *fall by the sword*, etc.; but at the end of the period *holiness will be justified*, which is the opposite of *truth being cast on the ground*. This may mean either that Eliahu will appear; or that Israel will enter their land from 'the wilderness of the Gentiles.' Probably, part of the 2300 falls in the time of the Arms, and part in the 'time and times;' since during that time, Israel will depart into 'the wilderness of the Gentiles' (*v. supra*). It is clear, therefore, (1) that *they will fall by the sword* before the *times*; (2) that part of the 2300 falls in the time of the Arms and part into the general sum of the *times*. Now, we have shown above that Ndf means a single time, and that Nyndf refers to periods *more than one*, not necessarily *two*. Most probably, this period is the same as that mentioned in ver. 11, *ubi vide*.

Breaking in pieces the power of the holy people refers to the tribulations that fell on Israel during these years. Observe that there is a time when tribulation will be on Israel only, and a time when tribulation will be on the whole world. See Jeremiah 30.5, where *we have heard a voice* refers to the news that will reach Israel, cp. Isaiah 24.16; and *fear and not peace* refers to tribulations which will be common to the whole world; cp. Isaiah 1.50,17, Jeremiah 1.6, 'Therefore I see every man with hands upon his loins,' followed by (ver. 7), 'it is the time of Jacob's trouble.' The last verse may indicate one of two things: either what will happen to Israel in the time of the Arms, mentioned above, which will be a *time of trouble*, or what will happen to them after they have entered their land from the 'wilderness of the Gentiles;' in which case it will refer to three events:

(a) What will come upon them from the 'northern,' see the comments on 11.44.

(b) The tribulation mentioned in Psalms 83, which refers to the 'tents of the Edomites and Ishmaelites.'

(c) Gog, the last tribulation that will befall them.

The order of tribulations then will be--(1) in the time of the Arms; (2) from the northern king; (3) from the 'tents of Edom; (4) Gog. During *all* these years the purification will go on; cp. Zecharia 13.9.

8. Daniel says, 'I heard the voice of the angel saying "for a time, times," etc., **but I did not understand**. He did not understand three things:

(a) He did not understand the length of a dfVm (v. on 7.14): dfVm, tf Ndf all three mean the same: a tf may be the twinkling of an eye, an hour, or anything more, e.g. years. The words *for a time* therefore conveyed no indication of a *definite period*.

(b) He did not know when these *times* commenced.

(c) The word *times* conveyed no notion of the *number* of times.

And I said, O my Lord: as much as to say 'I do not understand what you say: if you can tell me, what will be the end of these things?' The angel answered two things, (a) his question *what will be the end?* (b) his saying *I did not understand* (though the angel did not hear this last).

225

⁹He said, "Go, Daniel, for these words are secret and sealed to the time of the end.

9. **Are shut up**: cp. 8.26, 'shut up the vision;' only that was said to Daniel. This would not prove that no one else understood them [the words]. The words 'for they are shut up and sealed' indicate that they are hidden *from the children of men*.

Until the time of the end: until then they are closed. After that, they will be revealed.

He adds (below) that at that time many **will purify themselves**, indicating that the end will not come until after the purification of the nation from the transgressors.

Here we must pause a moment. Let us observe that there are certain texts that contain signs, the purpose of these signs is to point out the expected deliverance. These signs are of two classes: one consisting of the action of the nation, the other of the action of God. The first consists in our returning to God, the second in many things which we will describe. As for our returning to God, it is mentioned in the following passages: Deuteronomy 4.30, 30 Hosea 14.2, Jeremiah 3.14. Only they will not return to God until after great afflictions, as has been said before in this chapter, ver. 1. Cp. Isaiah 59.20.

Some of the Jews have been misled by Isaiah 8.16, 'And he saw that there was no man,' thinking that Israel perhaps would not repent, and that deliverance would come to them without repentance. This is an error. Could the deliverance come without repentance? If this were so, God would not have delayed it all this time. We can only say that the people of the Captivity at this point in time are divided into two classes: a good class, who will seek knowledge, multiply fasting and lamentation, put on sackcloth, and grovel in ashes, humiliating themselves, and asking God to deliver His people. Then, there is a class sunk in transgression,

226

submerged in the commission of capital offences, at the same time despising the pious sect, accusing them and looking upon them as hypocrites, excommunicating them and driving them away, because they will not assent to their doctrine, or adopt their faith. As for the first sect, they are those whose conduct is described in Isaiah 58.2, 'yet they seek me daily and delight to know my ways.' Where the author complains of wrong being committed in dealings and judgments between them and their poor, which they do not redress, and that they do not care sufficiently for the weak, see the chapter throughout. But to the mass of the nation, he says, 'Behold the LORD'S hand is not short so that it cannot save you. Your wickedness has separated you and your God. Your hands are defiled with blood,' down to 'truth is lacking' (ver. 15). It is to this verse that the words 'He saw' that **there was no man** refer. The words 'therefore his arm brought salvation to him' are a prophecy of troubles which will overtake these evil-doers until some of them repent, and the rest die. The possibility that the whole nation will repent is highly improbable. To the first sect he says, 'Hear the word of the LORD, you that tremble at His word;' where he tells them that their brothers hate them and revile them, saying at the same time, 'God is pleased with us, and for our sake the redemption will come;' in which they are deceived. This, then, is a partial account of what has been told us about their return to God, after which the redemption will come. A partial account, too, has been given on ver. 4. Let us now explain Israel's conversion to God, what will be done by their leaders and the masses.

The leaders will turn to the Law when they have come into the most miserable state of poverty, and their enemies among the nation and the great sect are most numerous.

They and their followers are the *people whose way is perfect*. The great sect will decline, those who follow the sayings of their predecessors. One after another will confess, until the two thousand three hundred days begin. At the time of the destruction of the thrones of the dynasties, when the people are merged in the *tribulations*, the doctrines of the leaders of the Jews will be discredited, as well as their authority. At that time, the enemy, the temporal LORD, will seek them out. Then, too, it will become clear to the multitudes, who accept their authority, that the truth is with the pious sect, and that through it the redemption will come. They will return to the Law and abandon the tradition of those who cling to the books of their ancestors. Then, God will no longer delay the redemption. This we have fully and satisfactorily explained in the Commentary on Chronicles. It would be too long to repeat it here. This is what we are told about *our* action.

What is told to us of *God's* action may also be divided into two parts. One refers to our condition prior to the redemption at our repentance. This is recounted in Deuteronomy 32. There, it is said that 'the LORD will judge His people,' that God will take revenge for His people upon their enemies. It goes on to say that He will forgive them when they are at the height of their trouble: 'when He sees that their power is gone.' This refers (1) to the weakness of poverty, (2) to the fact that there are no royal ministers among them who looked after their affairs, as there were when they had judges, governors, etc. Because of this, they became poor after having been rich from the wealth of their rulers and merchants; and they resigned their possessions: v. Zecharia 8.10. This is the meaning of *their power is gone*; to which is added, 'and there is none shut up or left at large:' i.e. none of them has power to bind or loose any more. The second refers to the condition of the Gentiles: *ibid.* 35, 'Vengeance is mine, and reward;' indicating that so long as the affairs of the Gentiles are well regulated, we will remain in our suffering, and our Captivity. However, when their fortunes begin to be reversed, their distress will come, and they will die quickly, 'for the day of their calamity is at hand.'

There are three signs of salvation. When they appear, the wise will know redemption is at hand. Therefore, he says **they are sealed and closed until the time of the end**. When the end approaches, it will be revealed. God in His mercy has seen fit to hide it from them; because, if they had known how long the Captivity was to last, multitudes of the people would have perished [apostatized]. Therefore, He left them in hope, expecting the deliverance. One after another will be converted, and God's anger will cease. When the time comes, these signs will appear, and they will know that the time has finally come. They will cling to their faith, except a few, as we said above.

¹⁰Many will be purified and purged and refined; the wicked will act wickedly and none of the wicked will understand; but the knowledgeable will understand.

10. **Many will purify themselves**: the people are divided into three classes, excluding a fourth, as I will now explain. He said above (11.35) **to refine them and to purify**; that is repeated here, to show that it is to be at the time of the end. **Purify** literally means *winnow* or *sift*, e. g. *grain* from *chaff*, *stones, earth*; cf. Jeremiah 4.11; or as the money-changer separates the good Dirham from the bad, or clears the good from the bad mixed up with them. The meaning is: among the people there are some who are good and repentant -- the wheat. There are also wicked ones who eat unlawful food, change Sabbaths and festivals, commit abominations, and do not repent. God will distinguish between them by destroying the bad, some of whom will die by the sword, others by pestilence; *v. supra,* and compare Ezekiel 20.38, Amos 9.10. As yet, we have two classes, the perfectly righteous, and the completely wicked. Now he says **and will make themselves white**, with reference to a class who are intermediate in religion, who keep the commandments, but not perfectly, being like a garment which has stains, and requires cleaning. So it must be washed; cp. Isaiah 64.5. When the tribulations come near, they will discard their sins; cp. Jeremiah 11.22. The intermediates are a stage below those of whom it is said **they will purify themselves**, the latter being perfectly righteous. These are descriptions of the people who will come out of the great sect.

And be refined: a description of the great sect themselves, who are compared to silver or gold mixed with *dross,* i.e. the doctrines which they have inherited from their fathers, so that they go along with what their leaders tell them, and affirm it. They will undergo tribulations. God will *refine* them, so that they will discard these doctrines and return

230

to the Law of YHWH. This describes their state shortly before the appearance of Elijah, as we have explained elsewhere (i.e. in the Psalms).

But the wicked will do wickedly: i.e. those that do wickedly against m the covenant (11.32). They are the portion to whom I alluded on the words 'they will purify themselves.' He means they will transgress more and more, and not understand, i.e. pay no regard to that which is written in the Book of God, in which case they might have turned to God, or might never have abandoned His religion. They are the people who *allegorize the text*, as we said before.

But those who are wise will understand: they will turn to the Book of God, understand its contents, and know that what God said in His Book has come to pass. Understanding that, they will make Israel understand it, who will then cling to the Law and throw off the sins that are upon them; *they will be strong and do exploits* (11.32).

(¹¹From the time the regular offering is abolished, and an appalling abomination is set up—it will be a thousand two hundred and ninety days. Happy the one who waits and reaches one thousand three hundred and thirty-five days.)

11. The angel now explains to him what he did not understand in ver. 7 (*v. supra*); showing him that a **time and times** refers to twelve hundred and ninety days. A **time** is restricted to a year, and **times** to two years. A **half** is something less than a year. Further, of this sum of four years all but a fraction *commences from the time that the continual will be removed. The continual* has now been mentioned three times, of which the first is -- 'It took away from him the continual, and the place of his sanctuary was cast down.'

There, he did not state who does this. Later on, he says that it is to be done by certain rulers, *arms from him will stand up* (11.30). He adds that 'they will profane the sanctuary and make the abomination desolate.' He repeats this here last, to show Daniel, and us, that the *times* start from the time of the removal of the *continualls* and that at the end of the twelve hundred and ninety days the tribulations will be ended. This he explained to Daniel.

Now, we must give the reason why he says *a time, times, and a half* with the word *time* once in the singular and once in the plural, instead of saying *three times*. We will answer this question as best we can. These times being *years*, as we have said, begin with the time of *the removal of the continually*. Isaiah's *three years*, as we said, are identical with the *time and times*. At the end of one year of these three, Isaiah tells us, 'the glory of Kedar will cease, and his warriors will be few;' that year is therefore the *time*, distinguished here as the first year of the three, where 'the whole glory of Kedar will die.' The other two years (or *times*) will be of one theme, viz. in them 'the glory of Moab' will finally be 'brought to contempt.' Isaiah does not speak of the *half-year* because it is in the time after

232

the fall of Ishmael. Probably, 'half' is an approximation. It is, probably, really more than half. It will last from the time of the conquest of Babylon by the king of the north until the time Israel enters Palestine from the 'wilderness of the peoples.' After this, the king of the north will die. Next, it is clear that *as the years of a hireling* refers to lunar years This will make the three years thirty-six months, or a thousand and sixty-five days, which will leave out of the twelve hundred and ninety days two hundred and twenty-five. This makes *half a time,* as we have said, the word ycH in the Hebrew language being used sometimes for an exact half, sometimes for slightly more or less, as we showed from Isaiah. Here, it is more. During this half-time there will be an excitement in the world caused by the king of the north. It will start from the time when Ishmael is destroyed and left without a leader. He will go out from Babylon until he dies in the land of Israel, as we have explained at 11.44.

¹²But you, go on to the end; you shall rest, and arise to your destiny at the end of the days."

12. These days are not the same as those mentioned above, nor are we told when they begin, or end. They do not come within the days of the kingdoms. The person who **waits** must already have got into the *time, times,* etc. He will then count them, knowing they are a short period, which will [soon] end, when he will be freed from the *tribulations.* Then, he will come to these thirteen hundred and thirty-five days. These people are the good, *whose way is perfect,* and their followers. Moses in Psalm 40 noticed this. At the end of that psalm he says 'with long life will I satisfy him;' doubtless, some people will die during the *time and times.* Therefore, he says blessed is he that waits and reaches, since not every one that waits will reach. Most probably, they begin from the destruction of the king of the north, when Israel will begin to prosper and their power increase. In them will be the second gathering of Israel, prophesied by Jeremiah (35.9). In those days the Messiah will appear and Israel will be secure.

At the end of those days God will come, and take vengeance upon him. That will be on the last day of the thirteen hundred and thirty-five. After God will be the reign of the Messiah over the people of the whole world. The thirteen hundred and thirty-five days are separated from the latter. There will be some troubles in the latter days, though they will be after the completion of the monarchies. Most of what we expect will come to pass in them.

He said above (ver. 9) *go Daniel,* without saying *where.* Here, he explains this: go, i.e. pass away. You and Israel, go to your grave in your sorrow, as the rest have passed away until the **time of the end**.

For you will rest: sc. in your grave; cp. Isaiah 57.2. We do not know where that grave was. Most probably, it was in Babylon. Daniel did not go up to the Second Temple, as

234

seems clear. In the third year of king Cyrus, he was in Babylon; whereas the Jews had gone up to Israel in Cyrus' first year.

You will stand: i.e. rise from the grave.

In your lot: either (1) the place of the reward which he had earned; or (2) the land of Israel, where he had a *lot*; so that he will live a long time at the redemption, and rejoice in the sanctuary of the Almighty and the reunion of the nation. After this God will take him alive to the place of reward among the angels. I prefer the second view.

Then he tells him *when* he will rise to be rewarded; **at the end of the days**: i.e. most probably at the end of the thirteen hundred and thirty-five days God will raise him up and bring him to his *lot*. At that time, too, the dead will be resurrected: 'Behold, I will open your graves, and cause you to come up out of your graves, O my people' (Ezekiel 37.12). Then, too, He will show them what He has promised (cp. Psalms 206.4).

Let us ask God Almighty to bring this near in our days and yours. Let us ask Him not to deny abundant knowledge of His Book, revelation of His secrets, and attachment to His faith. Let us ask Him to sanctify His sanctuary, and show us its restoration; *for the sake of his great name, and His abundant mercies*. Amen.

* * * *

We have explained this chapter in accordance with what we have heard from the teachers of the Captivity, or read in their books, so far as those theories seemed probable. God will forgive and pardon any slips or errors, in His goodness and gentleness. We will now follow this with a statement of the views of others about these times and the end that any one who cares to know them may. The scholars who preceded Joseph ibn Bakhtawi explained the 2300, 1290, and

235

1335 as *years*. The Rabbanites, too, spoke of the *end*, and thought that from the third year of Cyrus to the *end* would be 1335 years. The term passed some years since, so that their opinion has been disproved, and that of their followers. Similarly, El-Fayyumi explained it as years, and has been proved false. He had however some marvelous inventions with reference to *the time and times*. He was answered by Salmon ben Jerucham; whom we need not answer, since his term has past and the end not arrived. Certain of the Karaites, too, made the 2300 years date from the exodus from Egypt; that term too has past years ago, and their prophecy not come true. Salmon ben Jerucham, in his Commentary on Psalms 74.9, denied that it was possible to ascertain the *end*: but on Psalms 52.14 he offered a date which has passed. He agreed with many others in interpreting the 2300 and 1290 as days, but differed about the interpretation of the *time of the removal of the continual* which, he thought, meant the *destruction of the Second Temple*. Benjamin Nahawendi agreed with him in the later point, but differed from him about the days being days and not years. Benjamin took a separate view in believing that they were years. Salmon ben Jerucham referred the 1290 to the three and a half spoken of in chap. 10.27 ('for the half of the week He will cause the sacrifice and the offering to cease').

Each of the commentators has taken a different line, and all have gone wrong in making the days years. Benjamin Nahawendi, indeed, made the 2300 date from the destruction of Shiloh, and *from the time of the removal of the continual* from the destruction of the Second Temple. This leaves some 400 years still; but this is a delusion.

All these theories are confuted by two facts:

(1) Their inventors claim to know the *end*, the Scripture, however, says that the matter is *closed and sealed*. Any one, therefore, who claims to know it before *the time of the end* is

professing what cannot be true.

(2) They make the days years. Now we know that where he speaks of *weeks of years* he expressly distinguishes them from *weeks of days* consequently none of the three sums mentioned (2300, 1290, 1335) can be years. All must be days. The one commentator who made them days supposed the three periods to follow one upon the other; i.e. he made the 2300 the first *time*: the 1290 the second, the 1335 the third. He supposed there was no statement of the number of days of the *half-time*. He suggested that it might be half the first *time*. Assuredly, this is more probable than the views of the others.

We have now given the views that seem to us clear or probable. Let us now ask God to pardon any slips or errors; for what we have given is not any positive assertion, but merely a probability. The Almighty himself has said that *the words are shut up and sealed until the time of the end*. At that time it will be revealed by wise men. The *wise will understand*. God Almighty, in His mercy and loving-kindness, bring near their realization. Amen.

The Book of Nahum

Ch. 1.1. An oration concerning Nineveh, the book of prophecy [by] Nahum of Elqosh.

2. The LORD is Almighty, jealous and avenging, the LORD is avenging and the Master of wrath, taking revenge is the LORD on his enemies: and nourishing hatred for his foes.

Discussion of the five divine appellations occurring in the verse: The difference between enemies and foes consists in that the former are idolaters who oppress Israel, while the latter show no such hostile feelings. The former will therefore be punished by 'consummation and that determined' (Isaiah 10.23). This is an allusion to the authors of the troubles and is a repetition of the remarks on Daniel 12.1 *(Transl., p. 74)*

3. The LORD of the Universe is relenting in wrath and strong of power, but will not hold the guilty guiltless; the way of the LORD is in storm and whirlwind, and the cloud is the dust of his Shekinah.

The verse states that God puts up with 'the wicked' a long time, but eventually he calls them to account for what they have done to Israel. The words, *the way of the LORD, etc.,* can be explained literally as referring to the day of punishment. Speaking allegorically, the prophet compares the swiftness of the punishment with a gale. In that way, will he bring about their punishment quickly, 'when the time comes.' On that day, the daylight will be darkened as by a thick cloud. 'The first explanation is, however, preferable.

4. He rebukes the sea and dries it up, and he makes dry all rivers, Bashan and the inhabited world languish, and the summit of Lebanon languishes.
5. The mountains quake at him, the hills crumble, and the earth is upheaved before him, the world and all its inhabitants.

The allegorical explanation of this verse points to the

great kingdoms, Edom (Byzantium) and Ishmael (the Arabs) whose rule extends along the ocean over the world. Their armies toss about as the waves of the sea, but God rebukes them and destroys them. The *rivers* are the great *Emirs*. *Bashan* and *Carmel* stand for the generals, *Lebanon* for the royal princes, and the *mountains* for the other kingdoms. The first explanation, though, is more appropriate.

6. Who can abide his rebuke, and who can stand in the fierceness of his anger; his wrath is poured out like fire, and the rocks are broken by him.
The kings and warriors cannot withstand his anger. His punishment destroys the *wicked*.
7. The LORD is good, yea, a stronghold in the day of trouble, and he knows them that seek his protection.

God is jealous and punishes the 'wicked of the world;' but he delivers the 'pious and those who seek his protection' from 'the misfortunes that befall the wicked.'

8. And with an overrunning torrent he works destruction in their place, and darkness dogs his enemies.

Up to this point, the prophet speaks of the world as a whole, but all the following verses of the book relate to Nineveh. Should Babel be meant, then 'the torrent' refers to the ' Kings of the North' (see Daniel 11.40, 44).

9. What do you devise next to the LORD ? he is making a full end; disaster will not stand against you twice.

The people of Nineveh must not believe that God will only destroy one part of the city and save the other; he will destroy it all with one blow. Another interpreter says that he asks the people of Nineveh whether they think that God will destroy Israel, or that they (Israel) will meet with another [period of] trouble. The first explanation is much better. (See Driver, p. 22.)

10. For though they are [like] thorns entangled, and drenched in their drink, they will be destroyed like dry and completely parched stubble.

The people of Nineveh, after having reached the limit of oppressing Israel, will be destroyed like thorns by fire. The words *drenched in their drink* mean: As they measured out drink to other nations, so will God mete out to them the cup of intoxication. The last four words of the verse should be connected with the first four.

11. Out of you goes forth one who devises evil against the LORD, one that counsels iniquity.

The kings of Assyria went forth to destroy Israel. If this referred to Babel, the *Little Horn* is meant. The words *counsel of iniquity* may refer either to Sancheriv or to Babel, and the *Man of the Spirit*.

12. Thus says the LORD: since they are safe and likewise many, and even so will they be cut down, and it (their yoke) will pass away. I have afflicted you, (but) I will not afflict you for ever.

Israel, since you have seen the people of Nineveh free from calamities and numerous, let this not trouble you. They will certainly be cut off from their kingdom. Their yoke will be removed from your neck. If I have oppressed you long through them, I will do so no more.

13. And now I will break his yoke from off you, and your bonds will I cut.

He will break their yoke, which is upon Israel, and deliver them from paying tribute and tax.

14. And the LORD commands concerning you, no more of your name will be sown for ever; out of the house of your idol will I cut off the carved image and the molten image; I will make your grave, for you art vile.

The verse is addressed to the counsel of iniquity (ver. 11). The memory of his seed will be cut off. If this is taken as referring to the past, the verse refers to Sancheriv and his death in the temple of his God (2 Kings 19.37). If, however, this verse referred to the Little Horn, the verse speaks of the Arabian rulers of Bagdad, and of the descendants of the Man of the Spirit [Mohammad]. **The house of your idol** refers to their holy shrine to which they make pilgrimages every year. The words **it will make your grave** may also be referred to the time when the pilgrims travel, and the ' Arms' will rise against them, and slaughter them.

II.

1. Behold on the mountains the feet of one that brings good tidings, who announces safety; keep your feasts, 0 Judah, perform your vows; for the doer of evil will no more pass through you, he is utterly cut off.

If taken in the past tense, the verse refers to the failure of the kings of Assyria to conquer Jerusalem during the time of Tzedekkiah, but if Babel is meant, then the verse refers to the future.

2. The scatterer has come over your face; guard your fort, watch the road, make strong the loins, increase your strength greatly.

Some commentators refer the verse to Nineveh, others to Judah. In the latter case the scatterer is Sancheriv. If Nineveh is meant, the scatterer is the approaching enemy (Driver, p. 28). The words **watch the road** may be referred either to Ninveh's enemy or, mockingly, to the town itself.

3. For the L**ORD**** brings back the power of Jacob, as the power of Israel; now they have overthrown them and destroyed their cities (?).**

If the scatterer is the enemy that marches against Babel (Bagdad), then the words **the L****ORD**** brings back** agree with the opening words of the chapter. God will bring salvation by the Messiah who is the might of Jacob.

4. The shield of his mighty men is [of] red leather, men of valor, crimson through the glare of the torches; [so are] the chariots on the day when they are ready [for battle], and the shafts of the spears quiver. (See Ibn Ezra.)

The verse describes the equipment of the approaching enemy with their iron-proof shields of red leather and their coats of mail of the same color. The glare of the torches can be taken either literally or figuratively, meaning that the chariots are glittering with polished weapons like fire. The shafts that quiver can refer to the spears, but may also mean that the leaders of either army tremble.

5. The chariots rage in the streets, they overflow in the roads [or they clatter], their appearance is like torches, like lightnings do they run.

Having conquered the city, the enemy fills the streets, roaring like mad men, not caring whom they slaughter.

6. He remembers his grandees, they stumble in their march; they rush to the walls of the city, and the fortification is made secure.

This verse can be referred to the enemy as well as to the people of Nineveh. In the present case it is the attacking

king who, having entered the city as victor, inquires into the whereabouts of the generals of Nineveh, whose fame had inspired him with fear. They stumble in their march on account of the large number of slain as intimated in 3.3. **The fortification is made secure** means the distribution of armed men on the pinnacles of the walls. If the verse refers to Nineveh, it conveys that the generals are gathered together and lead their troops against the enemy, but in the confusion they stumble (see Ibn Ezra). The first explanation is better established (see Driver, p. 3x, who refers it to the 1 See Introduction, p. 4, and Plessner, Biblisches ,. Rabbin., p. 49.)

7. The gates of the rivers are broken through, and the palace is demolished.

The 'gates' are the openings in the wall made by the Tiglis, which enabled the enemy to conquer the city (see Driver, p. 32). As a consequence the inhabitants of the palace are heartbroken.

8. And he (the king) is pinned to the ground, while she (the queen) is driven forth and marches, and her maidens urge her gently on as it were with cooing tones, beating their breasts.

The king is lying on the ground, pierced by an arrow, while the queen is being brought into the country of the enemy. Her maidens urge her gently on, because she is pampered and not accustomed to put her foot on the ground. They all sigh and beat their breasts.

9. And Nineveh is like a pool of water from of old; yet they flee. 'stand, stand.' but no one turns.

Nineveh is as full of people and wealth as a pool is full of water.

10. Take you the spoil of silver, take you the spoil of gold, there is no limit to the stores, greater than any coveted furniture.

The *stores* are the arsenals filled by the kings. The sack of the city is valuable because it was the residence of kings and merchants.

11. Desolate, void and wide open is she, with a melting heart and loosened knees; tremor is in all loins, anti on all faces is the blackness of the pot.

Her village's streets are desolate, the fortress gates have been torn open. The fugitives are so panic-stricken that they are not able to flee, and blacken their faces (Driver: are waxed pale).

12. Where is the den of the lions, and the lion's feeding-place unto which the lion and the lioness and the lion's whelp go: and no one troubles them ?
13. A lion tears enough for his whelps, and strangles for his lionesses, he fills his caves with prey and his dens with rape.

The Kings of Nineveh are compared to savage beasts. If applied to Babel, the words refer to Nebuchadnezzar, and to certain Persian anti *Arab* rulers, *feeding-place unto which the lions* means that they absorb, a form of tribute, the substance of other countries.

14. Behold I am (coming) against you with revenge, says the Eternal God, I will burn their chariots in the smoke, and the sword will devour your young loins; and I will cut off your prey from the world, and the voice of your messengers will no more be heard.

Refers to the slaughter of the troops and kings. The messages that carried the king's commands to the provinces and collected the tribute will be cut off.

III.

1. the bloody city, all whose inhabitants are infidels: she is full [of injustice], robbery does not depart from her.

The kings of Assur and Babylon have shed innocent Israelite blood. All her inhabitants practice idolatry. This can be referred to their belief in God, his prophets, and his law, because though the *Little Horn* externally professes the Unity of God, it practices apostasy in different ways. Another explanation is that they rob the people's property.

2. The sound of a whip and the noise of wheels and stamping horses and chariots and rearing steeds.
3. Horseman mounting, and the flashing of the sword, and the glitter of the spear, and the multitude of the slain, and the heap of corpses, they stumble over corpses.

These two verses concur with 2.4.

4. Because of the multitude of the sin of the harlot, who is of rich beauty and enchanting; she sells nations by her extravagance and families by her witchcraft.

This is explained in the direction of Babel, the verse describes the alluring ways of the *Little Horn* and its armed strength, by means of which the king holds power as alluded to in Daniel 9. Its charm consists in the assertion that 'they possess a garden full of all that is good and pleasant.'

5. Behold, I am against you, says the Eternal God: I will lift your skirt up to your knee, and will show your nakedness to the nations, and your vileness to the peoples.
6. And I will throw loathsomeness upon you, and will make you like a leper.
7. And every one who looks at you will flee from you,

and will say: 'Nineveh has been despoiled. Who will bemoan her, where will I seek comforters for you?'

I will uncover the secrecy of her former conduct. She is like a harlot that first attracts and then repels. Thus, as soon as the way of the Man of the Spirit [Mohammad] is laid open and people know its baseness, they flee from it.

8. Art you better than the city of Alexandria which sits by the canals, water surrounds her. [she] who is a wall to the sea [rather] than the sea is a wall to her.

Nineveh, being surrounded by the waters of the Tigris, and by walls on the hind side, the prophet asks her if she is stronger than Alexandria.

9. She to whom Ethiopia and Egypt, gave strength, and without limit, and the people of Taft and Nubia did assist you, O Nation.

The last part of the sentence also refers to Amon in spite of the change of the suffix, analogous to ver. 7.

10. She, too, is gone into captivity, her children also are dashed to pieces at the top of every street; they cast the lot for her nobles, and all her honored ones are bound in fetters.

The women and old men have been spared, but all the young men are dead.

11. You also, O Nineveh, will be drunken, you will be hid; you also will seek the stronghold because of the enemy.

You will be drunken with misfortunes, and not remain in men's mind, as was the lot of other nations. You will live in protection (dimma) just as Israel. [dimma is the condition of protection under which Jews and Christians live in

Moslem lands by paying the poll-tax.]

12. All your castles will be [like] fig trees with the first ripe fruit; when they are shaken they fall into the mouth of the eater.
13. Behold your people are like women in the midst of you; the gates of your land have been conquered by your enemies, fire has devoured your bolts.

Your people have neither courage nor discernment nor fighting power.

14. Get you water for the siege, strengthen your castles, go into the clay, tread the mortar, take hold of the brick mould.

Although the verse speaks in the imperative it is to be understood that the people of Nineveh have done all this.

15. There will the fire devour you, the sword will cut you off, it will devour you tike the fly; make yourself heavy as the fire make yourself heavy as the locust.

The prophet compares the burning of the city, and the slaughter of the inhabitants with the destruction caused by the fly, which devours everything completely. The last words of the verse contain a satirical advice to collect a large army.

16. You have multiplied your merchants above the stars of heaven, the fly descends and disappears.

You have produced many merchants who brought you many goods. Do you imagine that they will last all the time? No, they will be like the fly which descends *to* the ground, fills it, but after a time disappears so completely that not one remains. Thus all those merchants who visit you will depart each one to his city.

17. Your saints are as the locusts and your patriarchs are like grasshoppers that alight on the walls in the cold day; but when the sun rises they fly away, and their place is not known, where they are.

Nineveh's nobles and wealthy citizens will fly away like these locusts.

18. Your shepherds slumber, O King of Assur; your chiefs are at rest; your people have taken flight upon the mountains, and there is none who gathers them:

The shepherds are the king's viziers.

19. Your hurt does not abate, painful is your wound, all those that hear your tale clap the hand over you; for upon whom have not disaster come from you continually?

Which are the nations and kings who have not continually drunk from your cup.